T0103646

So You Want to Be a Landlord

*A Practical, No-Nonsense Guide to Buying,
Selling, and Managing Low-Income Rental Property*

Michael J. Margolis

Order this book online at www.trafford.com
or email orders@trafford.com

Most Trafford titles are also available at major online book retailers.

© Copyright 2014 Michael J. Margolis.
All rights reserved. No part of this publication may be reproduced, stored in a
retrieval system, or transmitted, in any form or by any means, electronic, mechanical,
photocopying, recording, or otherwise, without the written prior permission of the author.

Printed in the United States of America.

ISBN: 978-1-4907-2832-2 (sc)
ISBN: 978-1-4907-2831-5 (hc)
ISBN: 978-1-4907-2833-9 (e)

Library of Congress Control Number: 2014903279

Because of the dynamic nature of the Internet, any web addresses or links contained in
this book may have changed since publication and may no longer be valid. The views
expressed in this work are solely those of the author and do not necessarily reflect the
views of the publisher, and the publisher hereby disclaims any responsibility for them.

Any people depicted in stock imagery provided by Thinkstock are models,
and such images are being used for illustrative purposes only.
Certain stock imagery © Thinkstock.

Trafford rev. 02/17/2014

 www.trafford.com

North America & international
toll-free: 1 888 232 4444 (USA & Canada)
fax: 812 355 4082

This book is dedicated to my parents, without whom I would not have received the confidence, background and education necessary to achieve many things in life, including this book. To Marla, my wife, for your steadfast support and contribution to the book. Your partnership in life and real estate is an ongoing one.

CONTENTS

Introduction xi

No Money Down? No Such Thing! 1

Why Property Investing? 3
    Politics of Property Investing 5

The Ugly 6

Income Property vs. Your Home 10
    Mr. Fixit 11
    On-site Manager 12
    Maintenance and Materials 13
    Security 14
    Taxes 16

Identify Your Property 17
    Research, Research, Research 19
    Style of Property 20
    Be Prepared to Negotiate 20
    Financing Options 22
    Home Equity 23
    Mortgage Products 24
    Existing Equity vs. No Equity 26

Purchase Wisely—Effective Valuations..................................27
    Comparative Approach 27
    Rental Income Approach....................................28
    Capitalization Rate vs. Gross Rent Multiplier....................29
    My Personal Approach 29
    Purchase and Sale Agreement (aka P&S)............................30

Protect Yourself and Your Tenants 31
    Environmental Hazards 31
    Lead Paint... 32
    Urea-formaldehyde Foam Insulation 33
    Mold and Mildew 34
        Insect and Rodent Infestation 35
        Presence of Possible Oil or Fuel Spills 37
        Bad People 37

Management and Operations **38**
    Renting Your Property and Finding Tenants 39
    Prepare the Apartment 41
    Rental Agreement...42
        Month-to-month aka Tenant-at-will 42
        One-year Lease 42
        Fundamentals of Lease...43
            Landlord/Tenant and Rental Amount..............43
            Financial Terms...44
            Remaining Terms...46
    Inspector Syndrome 47
    Rental Increases 49
    Create Good Habits 50
    Bookkeeping 50
    Cash Flow 51

Additional Income...**52**
    Tax Benefits of Investing.. 52
        1031 Tax-deferred Exchange 52
        Mitigation of Tax...54

Cell Sites, Billboards, and Profitable Entities 54
Cable and Telephone 55
Laundry Machines 56
Pet Fees 56
Storage Fees 57
Parking Fees 58
Utility and Government Programs 58

Cover Your Assets **59**
Limited Liability Corporation (LLC) 59
   Legal Work and Documentation 59
Evictions 60
   Build a Network 70
Insurance 71
   Tort Torts 72
   Fraud 74
   Flood and Sewage 74
   Fire Inspectors 74
      Smoke Detectors 75
      Carbon Monoxide (CO) 75

Business Acumen **76**
Appendix A: Property Performa 77
Appendix B: Month-to-month/Tenant-at-will 79
Appendix C: One-year Lease 88
Appendix D: P&S 97
Appendix E: Collection Letter 108
Appendix F: Tenant Application 110
Appendix G: Maintenance/Work Order 112

INTRODUCTION

My father used to say I always wanted to run before I walked. While this does hold true, I equate my logic to working smarter rather than harder. I love and respect my dad who has done remarkably well for himself, working at the same CPA firm for fifty years. While I commend this work ethic and commitment toward working sixty hours a week until that ever-increasing age of retirement, my philosophy is similar to that of a successful company: create as many profit centers as one can, preferably passive residual income streams. My philosophy reduces my dependency upon any one job, government subsidies, social security, or other programs, which are rapidly depleting and grossly underfunded to support the generations to come. The information imparted in the following pages is from me and pertains specifically to low-income rental properties. I am not a lawyer, not a mortgage broker, not an accountant, not a tax advisor, and not a real estate broker. I am simply a property investor—someone who took a chance, purchased some rental property, and turned profits. I am someone who, after losing money in the stock market, decided to invest in rental property. This book is intentionally short since I have included only what I believe to be the facts that are integral to success. Also, my focus is on low-income rental property, yielding high-income returns and nothing else. If you are interested in buying expensive condos, strip malls, warehouses, foreclosed property, auctions, or anything other than rental property, buy another book. Foreclosure and auction sales are addressed briefly in this book, however, they are not the focus here.

I say "no nonsense," as my focus is not only on how to make money but on mistakes that can lose money—some mistakes which I have made and from which you may potentially learn. My reasons behind writing this book and publicizing my approach are multiple. I almost subtitled this book "Not a Get-Rich-Quick Scheme." There are too many people advocating quick returns on investment without providing the details, tax ramifications, and legalities involved. My approach is no-nonsense. There are no tricks, but there are best practices. With the plethora of investment personalities, get-rich-quick schemes, and no-money-down approaches, I decided to provide a fresh perspective. Unlike the success touted in these alternative methods, my approach relies less on renovating distressed properties and more on finding quality properties that require very little work so as to allow for a more rapid return on investment. I am also not advocating the buy-and-flip method through this book. Although this may have proven lucrative, it involves a higher risk than I am advocating through my process.

None of us has a crystal ball into the future. Nothing is more evident of this fact than the 2010 collapse of the stock market. With the demise of financial institutions like AIG, Lehman Brothers, Fannie Mae, Freddie Mac, Washington Mutual, Morgan Stanley, and Wachovia among others, and the devaluation of dollar and its reciprocal adverse effect on real estate, the time to invest in real estate could not be better. In our current economic situation, most of us remain dazed and confused by what could have happened to Wall Street. The current challenges for first-time buyers coupled with the financial lending environment provide ample growth for the rental sector. In fact, the predatory lending practices of the past decade have rarely impacted investment properties since one typically has to pay a greater percent of the property value than a typical homeowner. Where formerly it was easier to attain a mortgage loan for as little as 10% down in certain circumstances, it is unlikely that banks will provide such leniency in the future. Today it is more likely to see Loan to Value (LTV) of

70% on such properties, which would require that you pay down 30% of the cost of the property at closing. Therefore, a $1,000,000 investment property would require you to finance $300,000 out of your own funds and the remainder from a commercial lender. There still are certain specialized programs offered by Fannie Mae and HUD, which provide excellent terms and rates yet have contingencies that limit your rental pool to a certain demographic and have other restrictions dictating how your property should be operated. These are great products if you have both the means to obtain them and if you can pass their often stringent personal lending requirements.

It is no secret that the majority of wealth is tied to real estate. After experiencing success, my wife and I have become somewhat evangelical about real estate. Furthermore, this is a great way to build self-esteem, equity, and retirement for yourself and your family. If you are interested in a get-rich-quick scheme, put this book back on the shelf and pick up one of the many other books on the topic. I do not have seminars and progressive steps to my approach, at least not yet. What I have done, and my philosophy, is to provide a somewhat simple and realistic approach to property investing. Hopefully, you will see the benefit of property investing and try this on your own. Perhaps the greatest barrier to investing in property is overcoming fear. I am reminded of the Nike slogan from the 1980s—"Just do it." Whenever anyone incredulously asks me how I got into real estate, the simple answer is that I simply did.

No Money Down?
No Such Thing!

My father always said, "You get nothing for nothing." Don't be suckered into thinking you can purchase property without money. This is an age-old game of semantics utilized by the charlatans of real estate to lure in the poor unsuspecting masses of dreamers in society. The "no money down" property-purchasing techniques are, for the most part and in most states, illegal tactics that will get you in trouble. There are no shortcuts to purchasing investment property. Of course, one may agree to virtually anything in a contract. However, in order to secure financing from any reputable financial institution, you will typically be required to put down a minimum of 20% for an investment property with four or less units and 25% for greater than four units. Banks are in the money business and do not simply give it away. There are clauses and terms in all my loans from varying banks, lenders, and financial institutions that ask you to indicate if the property is your primary residence or not. If not, you will be subject to the terms of an investment property loan and the related interest rates explained above. If you indicate that it is your primary residence, you will be eligible for different, perhaps more aggressive, loan products. Consequently, if you fraudulently indicate that it is your primary residence when in fact it is not, you will risk the prospect of the financial institution advancing or calling your loan. In so doing, they will require you to pay off the loan immediately, secure other financing, or, worse yet, potentially foreclose upon your property. I have also seen situations where individuals will offer up for collateral other pieces of property or valuables in exchange for the investment property.

There are many creative ways of requesting that the seller retain a second mortgage, which, by the way, is not typically authorized by lending institutions. Since lending institutions often require you to show the trail of funds leading to purchase, you could conceivably structure a side deal with the seller in which the seller provides the down payment funds prior to involvement with the financial institution. The money trail will need to be transparent, and it will appear that all funds came from you. Such *side deals* are not looked upon favorably by lending institutions, as they would prefer all funds involved with the transaction be disclosed. You may run the risk of losing your financing commitment from the lender if this is discovered.

On one occasion, I held a small second mortgage to enable a buyer to purchase a building I was selling. This unscrupulous individual made the minimum interest payments until six months prior to the loan expiration date when they sued me with a variety of ridiculous claims with the ultimate intent to avoid paying the sum they had agreed upon at closing. In the end, I won and he ended up paying the sum owed plus attorney fees. All this stress would likely have been avoided had I simply rejected the second mortgage since there would have been no funds at risk. I have been approached by a number of individuals looking for such arrangements, and, as the adage goes, a bird in the hand is worth two in the bush. Always take the money over the promise.

Why Property Investing?

When practiced with a modicum of good judgment, real estate is safer than the stock market. The large moneymaking machine, that is Wall Street, with its numerous financial planners, which have sprung up like weeds, consistently claiming to build you a "wall of protection" through "dollar cost averaging," is using your money to make themselves rich. It is also not unpatriotic to turn away from the stock market where others control your money. It is no secret that being a financial advisor has become a lucrative career. You will pay financial advisors a percentage of your income, whether that is a percent of return, a fee for service, or some sort of loaded fund, on the gamble that they will manage your money better than you will. Perhaps they will; perhaps they will not. They will continue to tell you that previous results are no indication of future earnings; the caveat emptor speak for financial advisors. However, judging from the performance of the stock market to date, your return on investment is unlikely to be better than 5%. Real estate should yield conservatively better than 15% in your first year of investing with double-digit growth for at least the first five years. Beyond the speculative elements of the stock market in normal conditions is the current market replete with the likes of Bernard Madoff and other financial advisor Ponzi schemes. Wall Street epitomizes big business, so do not be surprised if your financial advisor promotes the market and dismisses these claims. If you lose your shirt in the stock market, you will receive a statement and the good faith pat on the back from your advisor that this is just a temporary hiccup in the market and that you can continue with your regular investment strategy. They will lure you with statements that the market always returns.

Unfortunately, while these statements may have been accurate for many years, the fact of the matter is that the current zeitgeist and political climate, hampered by the Obama stimulus and TARP packages, have resulted in the demise of the stock market as we have known it. Bill Welch, former CEO of GE and recognized as one of the greatest CEOs of the twentieth century, stated this phenomenon accurately when he indicated that for the past forty years, the US GDP has not increased by greater than 2%, yet under the Obama plan of "economic recovery," Obama projects a recovery in the next decade. I suggest that you take control of your assets and remove yourself from the roulette table.

Another benefit to real estate is its inherent insurability. However, by practicing the real estate suggestions in this book, you may better mitigate your risk of losing your nest egg through effective measures. After all, unlike the stock market, property is insurable. If you happen to have a pipe burst, a fire, a sewage backup, or many other unexpected occurrences, you will typically be compensated for the repairs and more. In addition to the increase in value of your property with time, you will also have a consistent revenue stream of rental income. Unlike the stock market, you may borrow from your property in the form of equity lines and second mortgages. There are added advantages to having property when you are looking to expand your portfolio of properties. Typically, when banks and brokers are analyzing you and your credit worthiness, they utilize the Fair Isaac Company (FICO) rating. You will be a better candidate if you have existing property. This will become increasingly more important as you attempt to purchase larger multiunit investment properties, as the banks will be looking for a track record of your experience. At tax time, you will be able to deduct most of your expenses. Finally, if you decide that you require your funds five to ten years from now, you may determine that it is more advantageous to sell the property and enjoy your success.

Politics of Property Investing

Whatever your political proclivities are, you will find that one of the few constants in this volatile economy is that of consistent need for low-income investment property. With a Democrat regime, the entitlements, also known as Section 8 and other various local housing assistance programs, will likely increase, resulting in added government-subsidized tenants. This ultimately means an increase in tenants who have fewer challenges in paying their rent. The adverse effects of this ticket would arise when selling a property since the Democrats tend to lean toward increasing capital gains.

THE UGLY

Being a landlord is not exactly glamorous. In fact, it can be downright trying at times. The following are examples of what I have experienced; most are scenarios, which occurred when I was inexperienced.

A number of years ago, I evicted a tenant to whom I will refer to as Julius, the quintessential bad tenant. Julius claimed there were multiple problems with his apartment, none of which existed prior to his occupancy. He violated his lease in a variety of ways. The first violation occurred shortly after Julius moved in. *Violation 1* occurred when I came to welcome him to his apartment and was welcomed by two dogs; one of which was a pit bull, and both of them were a violation of the NO ANIMAL clause on his lease. When I informed Julius of his violation, he began negotiating. "These are my puppies. They're quiet. They don't bother anyone . . ." In order to accommodate this new tenant, and to avoid having to search for another, I agreed that he could keep the dogs as long as they stayed in the apartment and he paid a pet fee (which may or may not be legal in your state). It was dumb on my part but, at the time, a concession I thought I could live with. Julius agreed to this condition. *Violation 2* occurred when Julius kicked open the basement door, causing damage to the door, door jam, locks, and doorknob. To make matters worse, he placed a clothes washer and dryer in the basement which is off-limits to tenants. He then proceeded to brag to the other tenants about how he kicked the door in (not the brightest bulb on the chandelier). My first question to him was "Were you in the basement?" to which he launched into a tirade about the electricity not working. He claimed that every time he turned something on, the power went out. Once I got Julius to admit that he had broken the door down, I told him that he was overloading his circuitry, that he should not be plugging multiple electronics into one outlet, and that he would be required to pay for the damage out of his security. I also informed him that he would need to remove his laundry machines from the basement. I filed a police report against him, and approximately one year to the date of the incident, I was summoned to court to finally deal with this knucklehead. The bailiffs escorted him into the court in chains directly from some local prison. Once in court, accompanied by my witnesses, I sat and waited a full day, only to be told that his attorney needed more time to prepare and that they were unaware of the witnesses present, who were all recorded by the court prior to this date. Rescheduling would require me to return on a different day, lose an additional day of work, and only hope that the witnesses would be willing to do the same. This is a realistic example of how our legal system works. Please take this experience as a lesson and follow the steps provided in this book.

I received a call from a tenant, indicating that someone had defecated on the door down the hall and the mess and smell was as you might imagine. My first response was to ask them to call the police. Second, I contacted a tenant who had done some work for me in the past to clean it and I compensated him.

The fire department called to tell me the fire alarm in one of my buildings was not properly connected to the fire department. In the city where my building is located, any building containing more than six units must have a fire alarm that dials into the local fire department. I made the necessary correction. Although it cannot be easily proven, it is my belief that a disgruntled tenant cut one of the wires leading to the fire box which caused the malfunction in the first place. Regardless of how this might have occurred, as the landlord, and in order to ensure the safety of all tenants, I was required to repair it immediately.

My insurance representative notified me of work required for the existing carrier to continue insuring the property. The work consisted of replacing a fence section and cleaning up someone's rear deck. The same representative called a short time later to inform me that my insurance carrier cancelled the policy due to observing a pit bull on the premises. There typically is no recourse when the insurance company removes coverage other than to replace coverage through another "sub-prime" provider usually at a higher rate. See the Section on Insurance.

An inspector from a housing agency inspected a unit receiving assistance, and then proceeded to walk through the building and surrounding area to let me know that I needed to remove an unregistered vehicle from my parking lot and any and all trash from the vicinity of the building, plug a hole in the laundry room, and replace carpeting and many more items beyond the tenant's apartment. He asked me to repair a lock on one of the exit doors, which was repaired and shortly thereafter vandalized. The inspector then returned to the building and began contacting as many agencies as he could to complain about the property.

Many situations occur in retaliation to eviction proceedings. While I was in the process of evicting a tenant, the tenant began vandalizing property and subsequently contacted the local health agency, which decided to conduct a *random inspection*. This inspection resulted in a notice to me that instructed me to repair screens and lights in the hallway within a couple of days and advised me that I would be fined $1,000 per day until they received notice that these items had been repaired.

Another tenant who was being evicted for nonpayment of rent decided it was retaliation time, *accidentally* fell down the stairs, and used an ambulance chasing attorney to sue me for *damages*. Of course, insurance covers such situations, but it is still a nuisance. This situation is covered in more depth in Step 7 entitled Insurance.

I bought a six family and quickly realized that three of the six units were occupied by a family of drug dealers. I approached each and informed them that there would be no dealing at this location and that I am in cooperation with the local police. After evicting one of the family members, the rest followed him out of the building.

Following the purchase of a building that was purported to be a hangout for gangs, I hired an off-duty police officer to patrol the building for two weeks, installed cameras, and provided the drug task force with keys to the building. The activity quickly diminished, resulting in a safer living environment.

Other miscellaneous incidents include when, many years ago, I was called to address the problem of two female tenants who were having sex in the hallway in front of another tenant's door. In addition, we have had two people who were not tenants, simply visitors, die in the apartments on two separate occasions, allegedly due to drug overdoses.

While these are not all consistent issues, they can and will happen. My purpose for enumerating these experiences is to simply shed light on some of the reality of property management. If you opt to invest, be prepared for a variety of scenarios. Hopefully, you will learn from both my mistakes and successful practices. I did not experience the majority of these issues until I accumulated more than ten units. As you scale your business, you will need to make appropriate changes to your approach toward operations and management of your apartments.

Income Property vs. Your Home

One of the most common mistakes I have seen in those who do not succeed with investment property is the perception that they must renovate and update all properties that are purchased. These individuals confuse the *investment property* with their primary residence. Shortly after the property is purchased, these individuals hastily sink money into renovations and beautifying the apartments, only to come to the revelation that they have not turned a profit. I dissuaded good friends of mine from purchasing an investment property for the very reason that they were unable to separate the investment from the property and therefore were unable to make any income. The only time I would make an exception to this paradigm is if the property were an expensive high-end complex where the rents justify the space so that the property remains profitable. Simply put, too much overhead means too little profit. The most important elements of the property must be working bathrooms and kitchens; a new coat of paint, typically white; and clean floors and polyurethane wood floors. The combined effort should not cost more than $500. I spend considerable time in Step 5, covering the elements of running a successful business. It is imperative that you understand as much as possible about effective rental practices and the items covered in this book prior to venturing out on your own. Here is your chance to learn from my mistakes and successes.

Mr. Fixit

One vital element to reducing overhead is doing the work yourself. The $500 it may cost to prep an apartment could easily be $1,000 to $2,000, depending upon the contractor. Typically, I will tackle most small carpentry jobs; replace ceiling tiles; and handle new linoleum floor work, wiring of switches, correction of and installation of sinks, doorknobs, and other minor jobs that can save thousands when hiring a contractor. Usually there are tenants who are capable and in need of work that would help defer costs of a contractor. I often use such people to do the easier less labor-intensive jobs. In contrast, when the job is large and detailed, such as that of a new roof or wiring a house, I defer to the bonded and insured professional. With the litigious nature of our society and the liability involved with some of these tasks, it is much more prudent to hire a pro. This being said, always get a minimum of three quotes before hiring a contractor.

Never trust the tenant to do the work. This mistake has occurred many times where a tenant will suggest that they know of someone who may do the work inexpensively or that they can do the work and want reimbursement for expenses. Many issues may arise from this, the least of which is the fact that the job may not be done to your standards. Greater issues include the following potential liabilities:

1. The work may be unsafe for the tenant and other tenants in the building.
2. The tenant, in the process of performing the work, may have an accident, resulting in injury.
3. The tenant may, if given the opportunity, tap electrical, cable, and telephone lines from other tenants.
4. The tenant may spend too much money on something that could have been dealt with for less.

5. The tenant may, in the end, claim that more compensation is due him than originally discussed, which will result in further heartache if and when presented to the court if served eviction papers.

In one particular building I owned, each time I entered the parking lot, it was as if the ice cream man had just shown up. Tenants were appearing with hands out, looking for the next job to do, and complaining that the previous work performed by one of their neighbors was shoddy.

On-site Manager

When a capable, trustworthy tenant is identified, this person is an invaluable asset. While they are on-site, they may fix minor problems that may arise without your realizing that such a problem exists. I have such a person that performs much of the minor work, for which I compensate him. The other option is to hire a worker first, making him a tenant second. We have had our best luck with managers found through employment ads rather than employing existing tenants. Managers are looking for *work*, not just a way to secure free rent. They end up being much more trustworthy, experienced and reliable and have a better work ethic overall.

There are many considerations to be made when using an on-site manager. For one thing, if the manager does not work out, you will be faced with the loss of a manager and a tenant. Additionally, if the separation is acrimonious, this person will have all keys to the property and could create a problem. If this should become a problem, there are many property management companies that may be hired. These companies typically charge a fee for all work performed, along with at least 8% of the rental income. Many will charge a month's rent for renting a property. Typically, property management companies have scheduled fees for just about any duties performed on the property. Beyond the rental percentage, management companies tend to pad the cost for every part purchased. For instance, if a toilet is to be replaced and costs $100, it would not be unlikely for the management company to charge upward of $300-$150 for the toilet and $150 for the labor.

Maintenance and Materials

When repairing, or replacing, apartment items, try to purchase consistent inexpensive yet reliable materials. Paint should be one consistent color, and carpets another. Pay attention to hardware store closeout sales and stock up on regularly used items when on sale. Occasionally the large hardware stores will have sales on light bulbs including rebates from the local electric company. As indicated earlier, remember that this is an *investment property*, and do not spend time and money refurbishing. Tenants are especially savvy when it comes to improving their lot; if they find that you are replacing things in other units, they will soon be asking you to do so for them. This may be fine when it comes to light bulbs and occasional painting; however, when it comes to refrigerators, stoves, sinks, and toilets, this can become expensive. Be sure to obtain at least three quotes for every major job that you require. This will ensure that you're not overpaying for work, and you will get valued information from each contractor. I once had a plumber remove and install a new boiler at a building for a sizeable sum. When another property required maintenance, I had the same plumber quote the job. His quote was nearly 40% higher than the competitor that I hired. When I needed another job attended to and called the first plumber, he informed me that I should use the other guy because he was cheaper.

Make sure that whomever you choose as a contractor for any repair be insured. In order to validate that your property is properly insured, you should request that all contractors provide you with a binder from their insurance company that lists your LLC or property as insured. This will help to protect you from liability as a result of their work.

Security

Make your building a safe place to live. I have purchased buildings that have had gang-related activity, as well as drug dealers working in and out of the building. My first order of business is to move in the property manager. Once that trusted individual is in place, begin cleaning the property on a daily basis. This person will be your on-site eyes and ears. Immediately evict all non-payers of rent. If they haven't paid the previous landlord and are in arrears, they're not going to pay you. If you have a parking lot, issue parking stickers and tow all who do not belong, including unregistered vehicles. You will get a certain percentage of individuals calling you and complaining about this practice. My response is that if they had put the sticker on their vehicle as specified in the letter to them, it would not have been towed and that the parking stickers are for their safety, as well as others in the building. I have had tenants who use the parking lot as their garage repair shop and rental lot. Instituting these changes will put a quick end to these practices.

Install locks and keyless entry buzzers along with steel exterior doors. Just like an exterminator, your job will be to eradicate the filth and make it uncomfortable for drug dealers and buyers to conduct their business. If the behavior continues, 30 days after this consistent drug activity begins, hire a police detail sporadically for a couple of weeks straight, and if necessary on a monthly basis, to confuse and disorient the perpetrators. Meet with local police and officials to notify them of your objective to rejuvenate the property and that you will be assisting the city to eradicate crime one building at a time. Provide keys to the local police and allow access to your premises. Notify all tenants of what you are doing, and they will assist to get the word out that you are serious about improving their living conditions. In the event that you have a graffiti or vandalism issue, the best thing to do is to attend to the matter by immediately cleaning and repairing such damage. By doing so, you are sending the message that you care about the building and your tenants. Furthermore, tenants will have more pride in their living space when such activity is diminished. The combination of these efforts will result in a safer, more habitable environment for all involved. A safe building means a profitable building and one that attracts better quality tenants in the long run.

Taxes

Benjamin Franklin once said, "In this world, nothing is certain but death and taxes." Since I deal in people and not tea, I cannot simply revolt and throw them into the street, although sometimes it is tempting. In the city where I own property, the city levies a *personal tax* and charges fees for appliances in buildings with twelve or more units. Some tenants will be able to bring their own appliances, such as refrigerators which will alleviate the tax on those particular appliances. Most often however, if you are dealing in low income properties, tenants will not own, or have funds to purchase, their own appliances.

If you are wise enough to find multiple streams of income from the property, they will want to tax that too. Rule of thumb: do not publicize or speak about any additional profit centers for threat of additional taxation. For example, cell sites and billboards will result in an annual tax increase.

Simply put, if and when a property investor decides to actually make a profit, this profit will be taxed as a capital gain. If sold in under a year, this would be considered a short-term capital gain and taxed according to your income bracket, typically at 30% or greater. If sold beyond one year, this would be considered long-term capital gain and taxed currently at 15% as of the time of writing this book. I cover elements of tax later in this book, but it is important to understand the ramifications of the controlling political party and its impact on your money. According to Kiplinger's "State-by-state Guide to Taxes," printed in October 2013, where you live or invest determines the level of tax benefits or disadvantages you may encounter. In this article, he lists MA, OH, MT, and OR as "not tax friendly." These states are followed by the "least tax friendly" and include ME, VT, RI, CT, NY, NJ, IL, MN, CA, and HI. In contrast, the following states are listed as being "most tax friendly:" DE, WV, SC, AL, MS, LA, WY, NM, AZ, and NV.

IDENTIFY YOUR PROPERTY

I n the movie *The Super*, Joe Pesce plays a slumlord who is
learning the business through his father. In one particular
scene, his father is drilling him on the business of being a
slumlord and asks him in what situation he buys. The answer
of course is "death, divorce, and destitution." While such
circumstances will always exist, there are other items to investigate
when conducting due diligence on a potential property. The lion's
share of property investment capital is realized in the purchase
of the property. While there are multiple ways to enhance your
value, ultimately the initial purchase price is where you will make
or lose money. When becoming a rental property investor, it is
most important to identify the type of property you would like
to own, along with running a pro forma for determining future
income (see Appendix A). In this plan, such as the one contained
in this book, you should account for all possible expenses including
the loan amount. Any home that you intend to purchase that is
not your residence will be considered by the lending institution
to be an investment and will, therefore, require a minimum of
20% down payment for up to a four family. Therefore, when
starting out, I would recommend a four family. The difference
in cost between homes with four units and those with less than
four units is so negligible that it makes little sense to purchase
them. The return on investment with a four family will typically
be higher. Furthermore, in order to decrease the risk of vacancy,
more is better. When considering properties with greater than
four units, the down payment will be at least 25%. Although I

maintain my paradigm of 25% or less rental income paying for the mortgage, be sure to calculate for the higher percentage loan amount. Your best resource for calculating mortgage payments is the Web. There are numerous sites on the Web that will provide amortization projections and calculators based upon a variety of rates and products. The following Web sites may assist with your projections: www.bankrate.com/brm/mortgage-calculator.asp, www.mortgage-calc.com, www.mortgagecalculator.org, and www. interest.com/content/calculators/index.asp. I am merely suggesting these sites as a reference point, and in no way endorsing them.

Prior to identifying your property, you will need to determine your motivation for investing. Aside from the simple and obvious desire to make money, devise a plan of attack. Take into consideration the market conditions. Recently certain areas of the country went from emerging markets, showing high growth, to declining markets. One decade ago, Scottsdale, Arizona and Miami, Florida were emerging markets. Today, however, Scottsdale is oversold with declining values and Miami has been so overbuilt with large high-rise condos that there is a fire sale on much of the city. There is a great deal of speculation that Louisiana is a prime emerging market as the government is priming investors with advantageous products and tax breaks since the tragedy of Hurricane Katrina and ensuing flood of New Orleans. You need to be extremely cautious with such speculation. A realtor contacted me a few months back with a listing for a commercial purchase of a single-standing Starbucks. Given the rise and popularity of Starbucks, the investment which promised a 6% cap rate on a NNN lease, this appeared to be a strong conservative investment. Yet, a mere three months later, Starbucks announced mass closings of existing locations. How this might have impacted the investment is questionable but nonetheless is an important element of due diligence. Similarly, a large New England grocery store chain recently pulled its entire presence out of New Hampshire, leaving huge empty structures littering the downtown areas of many cities. One can only imagine what that is doing to the bottom line of that company.

Research, Research, Research

In the Internet age, you can research anything virtually, and real estate is no exception. Registries of Deeds are online, allowing you to search for when your identified property was purchased, along with all the activity that transpired for the owner or owners. This is essential in understanding the history of the building. For example, if you happen to notice that the property has been foreclosed or seized, or other notes indicating distress, this may signal some bad activity at the property. Go to the local board of health and request any reports or activity that has occurred at the property. Research the multiple auction sites for multifamily that may be offered for less. Work with numbers provided by different mortgage calculators.

A commonly used adage when purchasing property is "location, location, location." Although typically used to describe the value of a certain area and the quality of life, I would extend this meaning one step further to ensure that the region is investment-friendly. Know the area where you intend to purchase a property. Call the local police and request information on frequency of calls to the property and the general area of the property. Drive by the property at different times to gauge traffic and whether you would be comfortable walking into the building. Consult with mortgage brokers, attorneys, and other landlords. Most professionals would be happy to provide you with free advice on a particular area and building. Stop by and ask a tenant what it is like to live in the area. One constant is that there is no shortage of tenants who want to talk about their surroundings, the landlord, the other tenants, and so forth. I have had situations where my mortgage broker informed me that another property investor passed on a building I was looking to purchase. I then contacted the investor who gave me the history and rundown of the building. It turned out that this was not the type of building he was interested in and that he did not like the tenancy mix. I, however, have a different objective, and this building fit well within my goals.

Another important factor in owning property is being familiar with the laws of the land. The Housing Court's judge presiding over cases where I own is extremely pro-tenant. This judge has made it abundantly clear, and has indicated on multiple occasions, that it is the responsibility of the landlord to conduct proper screenings of tenants. This judge consistently dismisses the actions of landlords regardless of how heinous their nature, due to landlords who conducted improper process. Whether this is due to the climate of the region or an individual trait, I cannot overemphasize the importance of this element. There will be tenants who will not pay rent, will linger in the property, will do drugs, and will claim they are ill, injured, and incapable of paying their rent. Despite such promises, the law is black and white. Because of such rigidity in the legal process, you must look out for your best interest, regardless of the excuses provided by tenants. For more information around legal elements and landlord best practices, refer to Steps 5 and 7.

Style of Property

When first identifying which property to purchase, when looking at multiple-level buildings, try to find those in which the bathrooms and kitchens are aligned above other units' bathrooms and kitchens. In other words, each apartment has an identical footprint where units are stacked on top of another. Due to the potential leaks that may occur, this style of property will contain leaks in areas that will be less prone to damages.

Be Prepared to Negotiate

Prior to negotiating a price for the property in which you are interested, perform the steps listed above. Knowledge is power.

Armed with the valuation approaches and knowledge of expenses, you may better approximate a fair value for the property in question. Once you have evaluated your figures, then present an offer based upon your research. Never allow emotions to get in the way of good negotiation. If the figures do not work for your plan, you must not purchase the property. Always present an offer below asking price while bearing in mind the assessment figures. Before presenting the offer, do your best to analyze the seller and his or her motivation for selling. Questions that you may ask might include the following:

1. How long has the property been on the market?
2. Why are you selling?
3. How many vacant units are there?
4. How long have those units been vacant?

The next stage of the negotiation is to poke figurative holes in the property value by listing the potential problems and flaws from an initial walk-through. You will have another chance to nibble down the selling price upon inspection, but your first objective is to tie up the property with a reasonable offer. It is not uncommon to present an offer that is 30% below asking price. Be careful not to instantly employ this tactic since you will run the risk of not being taken seriously by the seller.

Yet another tactic to employ in the offer letter is that of contingencies. The more contingencies, the better protected you will be. Examples of contingencies might include the following:

1. Contingent upon inspection
2. Contingent upon financing of 85% loan to value or better
3. Contingent upon removal of oil tanks
4. Contingent upon lead inspection
5. Contingent upon exterminator evaluation
6. Contingent upon environmental evaluation

Contingencies will allow you to control the negotiation. Despite the results of these contingencies, you may opt to get out of the deal and not lose your down payment. It is your prerogative, regardless of reason, to pull out of a deal based upon your own subjectivity, feelings, or judgments. So, as ridiculous as it may sound, you may claim that you wanted a negative inspection, that you wanted to see insects, in order to pull out of a deal.

If you approach this systematically, you will find more success than failure. If your real estate agent or broker will not cooperate with such negotiation tactics, you may need to find one who will. If your offer is accepted, you will then hire a quality home inspector to evaluate and continue on the path of finding problems with the property. I always use someone affiliated with the American Society of Home Inspectors (www.ashi.org). Most owners are aware of the problems in their property, and when confronted with a reasonable expected cost for repair or replacement, they will typically concede to the inspector's findings. In this way, you will continue to reduce the cost of the property.

Financing Options

Financing your property may be achieved in a number of ways. The most common approach to purchasing a property with "no money down," which is commonly used by the TV real estate gurus of the day, is to use other people's money (OPM). Although I agree that OPM is a great way to fund a property, "no money down" systems are difficult to employ in many states and often rely upon a severely motivated seller. Therefore, it may take a long time to find all the variables required to make such systems work. In my estimation, the easiest way to find money is to use your own equity such as a home equity line. Home equity lines are tax deductible and generally have lower interest rates than conventional loan products. If you choose to use OPM, be certain that the terms of payback or compensation for such terms are equitable. Remember, time is money. If you are required to reimburse a party with an aggressive payment schedule, you may not realize the profit required to ensure your success. If you choose to run your own real estate investment company, be careful of the legal risks. Understand that if you are the manager of other people's asset(s), you become more than just an income property investor and effectively would become the general manager of a property management company. This is a large distinction as you would be accountable to property owned by others, which would result in legal ramifications and liabilities beyond your own. Be cautious of deals which seem too good to be true. Auctions and foreclosures could be an invitation for disaster. Closely evaluate the circumstances of the events which lead to distressed circumstances, resulting in auction or foreclosure. While in most cases purchase of a foreclosed property will require you to pay off only the first mortgage and not the remaining debt, the buyer usually assumes any and all liens on the property. Furthermore, unless you are given the chance to inspect a property prior to auction, which may only reveal surface-level details, you may be inheriting a disaster. It is not uncommon to find poor structural conditions, environmental hazards, bad roof, and other potential issues. If you are not a contractor and not willing to do extreme makeovers to your investment, I would stay clear of most auctions and foreclosures.

Home Equity

One of the best sources of funding for your investment property is you. If you own a home and have had this property for at least a year, chances are you may be eligible for a home equity line or loan. Borrowing from yourself could be risky if you have no plan to reimburse yourself; however, inherent to investment property described here is the ability to make money on your investment in a relatively short period of time. Typically, you will be able to borrow up to 75% of the equity in your home. Equity is determined by simply subtracting your mortgage or what you owe for the property from the market value of your property, as determined by the bank appraiser. For example, if your property appraises for $400,000 and you have a mortgage of $300,000, your equity is $100,000 and you would be eligible to borrow 75%, or $75,000, from yourself.

Appraised value ($400,000) – Loan amount ($300,000) = Equity ($100,000). This equity figure is commonly referred to as the loan to value (LTV) ($100,000) × 75% = $75,000.

Inquire of your local trusted financial institution for competitive equity rates. I have seen rates as low as 1.5 points below prime. Points simply refer to percentage. The prime rate, as reported by *The Wall Street Journal*'s bank survey, is among the most widely used benchmark in setting home equity lines of credit and credit card rates. It is, in turn, based on the fed funds rate, which is set by the Federal Reserve. The 11th District Cost of Funds Index (COFI) is a widely used benchmark for adjustable-rate mortgages.

Mortgage Products

Finding the right product for your financing needs is an art in and of itself. If purchasing anything beyond a four family, you should use a commercial mortgage broker or local bank. The reasons for this are multifold. Commercial brokers and small local banks are well versed in the most advantageous products on the marketplace. Commercial brokers and local banks deal with commercial property lending every day and are cognizant of the requirements to complete these transactions within the parameters set by the bank or lending institution. Commercial brokers have the benefit of working with multiple banks from around the world, which may offer further flexibility for your needs. Local banks know the valuation of your area and may provide more comfort in working with and speaking with the decision-makers. There will be many small or residential mortgage brokers who claim to be able to assist you with multifamily purchases, but I urge you to stay clear of these options for a variety of reasons. Fundamentally, residential mortgage representatives are typically unfamiliar with the guidelines and processes of financing a large property. Miscalculations that may result from using someone unfamiliar with these financing processes may result in not getting the financing you require, losing your down payment and other frustrating elements of inexperience. When seeking financing for one of my earlier properties, the residential lenders and banks were offering five-year notes amortized over twenty years with the requirement of 25% down. In contrast, the commercial lenders provided options for a ten-year note amortized over thirty years with 20% down or less, depending upon the arrangement of the financing as discussed in the previous chapter. Experienced commercial brokers will also be able to provide you with creative options to financing.

Other considerations for commercial mortgages are the prepayment penalties. Simply put, lenders make money when you buy and sell a property. The prepayment penalties may vary and depend upon the negotiation capabilities of you, your attorney, and those of the bank's attorney. Usually these prepayment penalties span a period of years, requiring a percentage payment of the full value of the loan balance within a specified time frame. For example, one of my properties has a five-year prepayment penalty with a percent corresponding to each of the first five years after the property is purchased. In the case of this example, I refinanced the property after two years, resulting in a 3% penalty back to the original lien holder. (5% penalty in year one, 4% in year two, 3% in year three, 2% in year four and 1% in year five of ownership.) Why, might you ask, did I refinance and incur this penalty? I was able to do a "cash out" refinance of the original property at a lower interest rate than before and, at the same time, take out substantial equity for the purchase of another building. This is as close to a no-money-down transaction as I can think of since, in this situation, I was not out-of-pocket any additional funds, simply a transfer of equity.

Due to the economic downturn, Dodd-Frank, and improper lending practices, lenders have become scrutinized to such a degree that finding effective multifamily lending options has become more of an art. I was able to refinance all properties with a local bank, which so happened to be in the market to expand their portfolio of loans in the multifamily realm. Not only were they extremely helpful, but they were able to provide lower rates than any other institution I previously had experience with and were able to refinance all my properties.

An additional consideration that you should look for when selecting your product is the option to assume the existing mortgage. In so doing, you will be able to transfer the property mortgage to a new buyer, assuming the new buyer qualifies for the financing conditions of the lender.

You should be aware that when purchasing a property of greater than four units, the fees and closing costs incurred for the transaction are higher than residential closing costs. Attorney fees, appraisal fees, and inspection fees are typically more than double that of home inspections.

Existing Equity vs. No Equity

If you are not fortunate enough to have existing equity to draw from, you are more reliant upon OPM. This process may also be referred to as cross-collateralizing. There are many programs available for people in lower income brackets. Research your local city and state Web sites for programs to benefit first-time buyers, or *soft seconds*, second mortgages, that are often extremely beneficial to the borrower. Many housing authorities advertise such programs. While it may be ill-advised to do so, depending upon your credit worthiness, you may opt to use credit cards toward securing the down payment to your property. This is extremely risky, and if you fail to make your payments, the credit card company will increase your rate of interest. So while this may assist you to capitalize your property, you will be at risk to paying usurious interest rates.

PURCHASE WISELY—
EFFECTIVE VALUATIONS

Ben Franklin once said, "A fool and his money are soon to part." The most critical moment of investing wisely is in the purchase of the property. At this point, you will set the stage for either losing money rapidly or earning money incrementally. I cannot stress enough the importance of conducting due diligence at this crucial phase of property investing. There are variety of methods for arriving at a property valuation, and they are most commonly the comparative valuation and the rental income valuation approach. In commercial properties, the square footage is used to determine value for a given area and type of property. Appraisals have become the most imperative element in determining valuations today. Appraisers are objective agents hired by the bank to perform an unbiased valuation using the methods described below. Keep in mind that due to the conservative nature of appraisers, they will typically err on the side of caution and provide the lowest valuation they encounter through the variety of methods employed. The following valuation methods are commonly used.

Comparative Approach

The comparative valuation is just a comparison of similar property sales that have occurred in a close radius to the property. Typically referred to as "comps," with this approach, banks will assign independent property appraisers who will search sales of similar properties within a one-mile radius of your property and which have been sold within the previous six months. The appraiser will match at least three properties and determine a value from these comps. There are many limiting elements to this approach. Fundamentally, if no similar properties have been sold, the appraiser must be creative in his determination. In my experience, the approach falls short when your property is newer, in better condition, and in a better area than that of the comps. Also, the recent influx of foreclosures will make your property seem too expensive for the market. Never sell in a down market. There will be many who will attempt to exploit this condition by telling you they could pay substantially lower for other properties in your area. This is a great tact for buying, but if selling, I would respond to such comments with the assertion that your property is devoid of environmental and other hazardous risks which will undoubtedly cost the buyer significant expense to rectify. These risks include, but are not limited to, eviction of poor tenancy, environmental issues, and multiple damages, all of which are covered in other chapters of this book.

Rental Income Approach

Typically, this is attained by first arriving at the *net operating income* (NOI). Simply stated, the NOI is the income generated by the property, less all expenses excluding the mortgage. The NOI is then multiplied by 10 to arrive at the value in this approach. For example, if a four family rents out at $1,000 per unit and happens to be occupied for a year, the rental income would be $48,000. If expenses for the property are $20,000, the net operating income would be $28,000. $28,000 multiplied by 10 gives you a valuation using this method of $280,000. Depending upon where in the country you are purchasing your property, this figure may be high or low. In the nicest areas, this valuation is ineffective since people typically will not sell for that figure, whereas in more depressed areas, you will be more apt to find a property below this figure. This further illustrates the fact that if you purchase a property in a high-end area, it will be more difficult to turn a profit, which is why I have focused my efforts on lower income properties in cities.

Capitalization Rate vs. Gross Rent Multiplier

Another term commonly used in real estate valuation circles is the *capitalization rate (cap rate)*. The cap rate is the price of the property divided by the net operating income. In the example above, a $280,000 sales price divided by NOI of $28,000 yields the resulting cap rate of 10. So the higher the cap rate, the better the deal.

The *gross rent multiplier,* the sales price of the property divided by the monthly income, will give you yet another assessment figure for comparing and contrasting property values. Using the figures above, if the target property is $280,000 divided by the monthly income of $4,000 ($48,000 annual income/12 months), this equals $70,000, which is also the cost per unit.

My Personal Approach

Real estate terms come in handy, yet in my initial investments, being unaware of much of the terminology in the marketplace, I was content in subscribing to the simple premise that I will be happy as long as the property earns more than I spend. In my case, I am somewhat more careful about maintaining a higher profit margin. If you are simply interested in riding the market by purchasing a property to sit on for appreciation, it is ill-advised, and you would probably be better served in the stock market since it is easier to swap funds than swap houses. For my personal guidelines, I prefer that 50% or less of the rent pays for the mortgage with the rest reserved for expenses and profit. In a later chapter entitled Rental Increases, I discuss the art of enhancing property return on investment (ROI). Although most of the ROI is established upon purchase of the building, there are many ways to mitigate expense and increase profits.

Purchase and Sale Agreement (aka P&S)

The Purchase and Sale Agreement is also commonly referred to as simply the P&S. This is the binding document used to purchase a property. You must be careful and research your local laws concerning the P&S as they do vary. In some states, the P&S serves as an offer letter, indicating the conditions of purchase and sale that lock one into the transaction, whereas in other states, the P&S is more of a formality, outlining the agreed-upon transfer of property ownership between the parties. See Appendix D which contains a sample P&S.

Protect Yourself
and Your Tenants

C aveat emptor, or buyer beware, is vital to your future in real estate. In order to best mitigate your risks in real estate, it is your obligation to find a property that is free and clear of obvious and not-so-obvious flaws and problems. Once you purchase the building, you are responsible for everything in that building. The following items are things to be aware of. Use them to nibble down the price, or simply walk away:

Environmental Hazards

Environmental hazards such as lead, urea-formaldehyde, mold and mildew, insect infestation, buried oil tank or possible leakage, previous fuel station or possible leakage are reasons for walking away from a property. Remediation of these issues is far too expensive in most cases to even consider a property with even a hint of the existence of any of these issues. Even if you can afford to make the corrections, you will be inundated with government officials watching over your shoulder every step of the way as many of these processes are strictly regulated by the law.

Lead Paint

Lead is an insidious poison that was once used in paint as a smoothing agent. This paint could be found on window frames, walls, the outside of homes, and other surfaces. The danger is that a child under the age of six may ingest flakes of paint that contain the lead poison. The poison will reap havoc on the child. This risk also applies to pregnant women as the fetus may be infected through inhalation of lead. You will need to be especially careful to whom you are renting, however keep in mind that it may be considered discrimination in some states to refuse to rent to a pregnant woman or someone with small children based on the existence of lead paint in the building The United States Environmental Protection Agency states as follows:

> Lead affects practically all systems within the body. At high levels it can cause convulsions, coma, and even death. Lower levels of lead can adversely affect the brain, central nervous system, blood cells, and kidneys.
>
> The effects of lead exposure on fetuses and young children can be severe. They include delays in physical and mental development, lower IQ levels, shortened attention spans, and increased behavioral problems. Fetuses, infants, and children are more vulnerable to lead exposure than adults since lead is more easily absorbed into growing bodies, and the tissues of small children are more sensitive to the damaging effects of lead. Children may have higher exposures since they are more likely to get lead dust on their hands and then put their fingers or other lead-contaminated objects into their mouths.

Lead was most commonly used in more upscale properties prior to 1978 when it was banned. However, in older regions of the country, there are still buildings where the owner is either unaware of the problem or, even worse, not disclosing the problem despite the legal obligation to communicate the existence of lead with the buyer and tenants. Moreover, it has become common practice for realtors to pass out the lead paint disclosure. Lead paint is typically found in and around old windows. Removal of lead requires a special process that is typically reserved for certified lead removal professionals. One may also take a course to acquire the skills to do so. In either case, it is extremely expensive and a nuisance to deal with.

Another commonly used method is encapsulating the lead paint so as not to disturb it. Although it is still legal to rent apartments with lead paint, it is not legal to rent to pregnant women or those with children under the age of six. It is in your best interest to confirm the age of such children using birth certificates, again keeping in mind that the act of doing so may be discrimination and may create a legal issue for you that you had not intended. If the building happens to be built prior to 1978, request lead compliance certificates from the seller. Aside from this documentation, do not take anyone's word on anything related to environmental hazards. More information on this topic may be found at http://www.epa.gov/iaq/homes/hip-lead.html. Additionally, you may find a booklet to print and pass on to your tenant at http://www.thelpa.com/free/leadpaint.pdf. I, personally, have chosen never to buy a property that has lead paint to simply avoid this rather tricky pitfall.

Urea-formaldehyde Foam Insulation

Urea-formaldehyde foam insulation (UFFI) is a form of foam insulation that has been commonly used in homes throughout North America for the past twenty years. Although it provided a great alternative to previous methods of insulation, it released toxins in the air that have resulted in a variety of ailments in those who were unfortunate enough to have inhaled them. Therefore, UFFI has been banned in many states. While buildings exist with

UFFI in tact, it is a vital point of inspection. The United States Environmental Protection Agency indicates as follows:

> Formaldehyde, a colorless, pungent-smelling gas, can cause watery eyes, burning sensations in the eyes and throat, nausea, and difficulty in breathing in some humans exposed at elevated levels (above 0.1 parts per million). High concentrations may trigger attacks in people with asthma. There is evidence that some people can develop a sensitivity to formaldehyde. It has also been shown to cause cancer in animals and may cause cancer in humans. Health effects include eye, nose, and throat irritation; wheezing and coughing; fatigue; skin rash; severe allergic reactions. May cause cancer. May also cause other effects listed under "organic gases" (EPA's Integrated Risk Information System profile, http://www.epa.gov/iris/subst/0419.htm).

Mold and Mildew

Mold and mildew are naturally occurring living things. Unfortunately, its presence can create a multitude of problems. The United States Environmental Protection Agency states as follows:

> Molds are usually not a problem indoors, unless mold spores land on a wet or damp spot and begin growing. Molds have the potential to cause health problems. Molds produce allergens (substances that can cause allergic reactions), irritants, and in some cases, potentially toxic substances (mycotoxins). Inhaling or touching mold or mold spores may cause allergic reactions in sensitive individuals. Allergic responses include hay fever-type symptoms, such as sneezing, runny nose, red eyes, and skin rash (dermatitis). Allergic reactions to mold are common. They can be

immediate or delayed. Molds can also cause asthma attacks in people with asthma who are allergic to mold. In addition, mold exposure can irritate the eyes, skin, nose, throat, and lungs of both mold-allergic and non-allergic people. Symptoms other than the allergic and irritant types are not commonly reported as a result of inhaling mold. Research on mold and health effects is ongoing. This brochure provides a brief overview; it does not describe all potential health effects related to mold exposure. For more detailed information consult a health professional. You may also wish to consult your state or local health department.

Mold and mildew may be readily recognized by a discoloration of wood surfaces. Typically, this condition is encouraged by moisture and poor ventilation. More information on this topic is available at http://www.epa.gov/iaq/molds/moldbasics.html.

Insect and Rodent Infestation

For millions of years, insects have roamed the earth. Bugs and rodents are everywhere. But most of us do not want them in our backyards. One of the most damaging insects is the termite. These are small, winged insects that swarm together. Termites are attracted to light and are often seen around windows and doors. If you happen to find them emerging from tree stumps, woodpiles, and other locations out in the yard, it is not necessarily a cause for concern and does not necessarily mean that the house is infested. On the other hand, if winged termites are seen emerging from the base of a foundation wall or adjoining porches and patios, there is a good chance the house is infested also, and treatment may be warranted. Other signs of infestation are earthen (mud) tubes extending over foundation walls, support piers, sill plates, floor joists, etc. The mud tubes are typically about the diameter of a pencil, but sometimes can be thicker.

Cockroaches are a further nuisance commonly found in unsanitary environments. They require ongoing treatment to mitigate continued contamination. Cockroaches, when treated in one apartment, may move to another. They thrive in walls and are prevalent in areas where food and water are readily accessible. Any potential infestation may result in a tenant declining payment of their rent. Under the laws of most states, tenants may withhold rent with evidence of infestation. The only thing a tenant would need to do is contact the local board of health to validate the presence of this vermin, which would ensure them additional time to withhold rent. In Massachusetts, a landlord may not pursue certain eviction actions for up to six months following the validation of such an issue. The savvy tenant will likely exploit this situation, which will be further addressed under the eviction section of this book. Once the extermination has been effectively addressed and documented, a 14-day notice may be more impactful toward removing such tenants should they continue to withhold rent or fail to pay the back rent. Laws in each state vary, so do not rely on this statement to be true in all cases.

Bedbugs are a common byproduct of poor hygiene. The tenant will certainly deny any presence of bedbug is the result of their personal hygiene. However, the bedbugs will cling to clothing, mattresses, and furniture. While such insects travel well, it will ultimately be the landlord who will be required to eradicate this issue.

Rodents may be spotted by their excrement. Small, open crevasses in walls invite such creatures. Health inspectors are quick to find such evidence. It would be wise to have a licensed exterminator on contract to perform regular preventative maintenance around your property. Not only does this create an ongoing safer environment, but it will provide a regular record of treatments to substantiate your due diligence. Also, with regular periodic inspections of your property, be on the lookout for unkempt tenants and be quick to admonish them for keeping unclean apartments that invite such nuisances.

Presence of Possible Oil or Fuel Spills

Be on the lookout for the potential buried oil tank or presence of fuel beneath the building. If it is disclosed that the building was built on property previously used for a gas station, walk away. Environmental laws are extremely rigid and unforgiving, especially when it pertains to the potential of fuel leaching into soil. Regardless of who was responsible for such a hazard, you will inherit the mess once you buy the building. There are cases where buildings have changed hands multiple times and all who owned the building in that time frame were responsible for damages.

Bad People

I have always believed people are generally good. When it comes to investments and maintaining your best interests, bad people or those who do bad things are worse than any other environmental issue. Bad people, or those who make bad choices, will not only create a bad environment for themselves and those around them, but they will ensure that they make as many problems as possible. Bad people will scare away good people. They may take the form of a drug dealer or prostitute who operates his or her business from the property. Such individuals create issues merely by performing illegal acts. In the process of their *work*, they will attract other seedy elements to your building. It should be noted that, while their actions may be illegal, you may not be able to evict a tenant based upon a crime committed outside of your property. Again, this will depend on the laws in your state. I had a tenant who I read about in the local police log, who happened to knock out an elderly lady with a rock and steal her money. As despicable as this act may be, you may not evict them for that action. You could, however, evict the tenant for using the property for illegal purposes. I cover more about evictions and bad tenants in the Eviction Section, but thought it made sense to mention here too.

Management and Operations

M anage your own property. One of the highest expenses incurred by those individuals who hire a management company is that of management expenses. As stated earlier, much of the work required on a property is maintenance that may be easily handled with a little work by the owner or an on-site assistant. Typical management fees can run anywhere from 8% to 15% of the total income of a property. Beyond the percentage, override is the added expenses charged by such companies for repairs. Many real estate books will advocate for management companies. In my experience, such companies may be good if you have found that you have too many properties to effectively manage on your own, and you trust that they will not be simply running up fees for every coat of paint and doorknob replaced at the property. Yet if you find that you have too many properties to effectively manage by yourself, you are probably doing well enough to afford a property manager.

On a regular basis, as you meet or collect rent from tenants, it is a good practice to take ongoing pictures of the units. This will serve as a record of the condition of the apartment. At the outset of a lease, you should provide the tenant with a property condition form to fill out and sign. See Appendix F. This condition form will address and confirm that everything in the apartment is up to snuff. If the tenant decides to create a problem by damaging and/or indicating that the property is deficient in any area, these practices will be especially useful. Any and all repairs should be requested of management by the tenant. See Appendix G.

Renting Your Property and Finding Tenants

Everyone needs a place to live. As I alluded to earlier in this book, my niche is lower income properties considered C+ or B-rated properties. Such ratings are for properties that meet inspection criteria, yet are often devoid of the luxuries included in middle-class to upper-class properties. With the decrease of interest rates and consequent increase of homebuyers in the middle-class segment, I have found this demographic to be the most consistent rental market. Many of my tenants are on Section 8 housing assistance programs, which are government- and state-subsidized rental assistance programs. The benefit of such programs is that they provide a great percentage of payment for those tenants in need. This means less collection responsibility on the part of the landlord and a greater likelihood that the landlord is paid in a timely manner. Moreover, as the landlord, you are not allowed to decline or discriminate tenancy based upon Section 8 status. When working with such programs, be sure to provide them with a W-2 form to ensure proper payment and taxation. An added benefit to government-subsidized programs is that you may elect from a variety of assistance programs offered throughout the state. Some agencies will pay more for rent than others. This is especially vital when dealing with a city or town that effectively provides "rent control" in there municipality. I have had certain housing authority inspectors inform me that they will not approve rent above a specified amount, based upon the region or section of the city or town, regardless of the amenities in the apartment. As for vacancies, there are numerous shelters and individuals who, while they may qualify for Section 8, may have difficulty attaining other types of apartments. If such tenants are delinquent in paying their rent, they may risk losing their Section 8, which is a further deterrent to nonpayment of rent. However, even this is no panacea toward getting good tenants. If there is a problem tenant, the housing authority will not assist you. If this tenant opts not to pay his or her portion, you may inform the housing authority, which could threaten their access to the program, but as for your apartment, you will need to deal with such individuals as one would any tenant. I have had some situations in which the Section 8 tenant damages screens and windows that were new only one year prior. Despite records and clean inspections from the previous year, the inspectors will still require the landlord to repair all such issues. Refer to the Section on Inspectors.

Tenants must understand that payment of rent is their responsibility, and that you should not be required to chase them down. One way to ensure timely payments of rent would be to set up credit or debit card autodraft for tenant rent payments. Autodraft will save you a great deal of time in the collection process. In my experience, I have found it difficult to get most people on the same time schedule for collecting rents, which would mean multiple trips to their apartment. Other methods of collection may be to have a designated, trusted, manager who may accommodate the tenants' schedule. But, be cautious of anyone handling large sums of cash. Alternatively, you could provide a mail box address for check or money order payments to be delivered.

Often my friends and I will joke and call me a slumlord. The fact of the matter is I am a landlord who owns buildings in low-income areas. The challenge of owning such properties is the tenant mix. One needs to be extremely careful when renting in these areas. People of low income typically have poor credit, which negates the effectiveness of a credit check. The best thing one can do when screening a tenant is to contact previous landlords. Do not necessarily contact the current landlord. Contact the landlord prior who has no incentive to give a false positive reference simply to get a bad tenant out of their apartment. Also contactwork references. If the person cannot provide any information, that is a red flag. In order to get around this obstacle, ask not whether the applicant was a good employee. Instead, ask if the applicant was on time each day, whether many sick days were used, whether he or she was always dressed neatly and was easy to work with. You may also ask if the applicant is eligible for rehire should they no longer be employed by this employer. Along with the work references, you will need to have all prospective tenants fill out an application, and from the application, you will need to gauge current salary and determine if, based upon the salary listed, this tenant can afford to make monthly rent payments. Additionally, if the person is not working, they had better have disability, housing assistance, or other reliable means of payment, otherwise you are flirting with disaster. Simply relying on child support or other funds not being paid by a governmental agency is a mistake you will regret.

Prepare the Apartment

Set the following best practices. Prior to occupancy, obtain an occupancy permit from the local municipal health inspector. Take pictures of the entire unit. Ensure that the tenant signs off on the status and condition of the premises and that everything is to their satisfaction. Each time any maintenance or inspection is requested or conducted, provide documentation of the event and have the tenant sign and date that such work has been completed. Without such verification, you will eventually find yourself defending against claims that such work was not done and that you were derelict in your responsibilities. Furthermore, such documentation will provide an ongoing log of repairs to the apartment and ensure that you are in compliance with various safety and maintenance requirements. It will also assist in managing expenses long term.

Rental Agreement

As one may agree to anything, there are certain specific elements of rental agreements that are enforceable by law and many more that a tenant will probably not contest. I have seen some agreements in which the landlord levied a fee for late payment of rent; some include clauses requiring the tenant to remove snow from their own steps. There are a multitude of sources for rental agreements including realtors, Web sites, lawyers, other landlords, and books. For the most part, apartment leases, whether they are month-to-month or a one-year lease, have distinct advantages and disadvantages.

Month-to-month aka Tenant-at-will

Fundamentally, if you are somewhat skeptical about a tenant's ability to comply with the rental agreement, if you choose to rent to this person at all, you should opt for the month-to-month lease. This allows you and the tenant the flexibility of deciding on a monthly basis whether or not the arrangement is mutually beneficial. With the month-to-month lease, you may evict a tenant sooner than in a one-year lease. This is typically not available with housing assistance programs since they will opt for the annual commitment. People who will take advantage of the month-to-month lease may not be interested in a committed living situation, may be more transient in their lifestyle, or may simply be looking for a temporary living solution. See Appendix B.

One-year Lease

One-year leases are less flexible than month-to-month in matters of eviction. Such tenants tend to be more committed and serious about their living situation. See Appendix C.

Fundamentals of Lease

Whether you are contracting for a month-to-month or one-year lease, there are certain consistent elements of a lease which will be discussed here:

Landlord/Tenant and Rental Amount

The following language identifies the most essential elements of the lease, to include all parties in the transaction, social security number of tenant(s), and pertinent information, identifying the specific apartment, address, and rent to be paid. Also you are indicating when the payment is to be received and the terms of the agreement, in this case "one (1) month." Also, that the landlord may increase rent with 30 days notice.

Date: _____

[LANDLORD NAME AND ADDRESS] rents and the

Tenant: _____ SS# _____

Tenant: _____ SS# _____

hires the premises at [PROPERTY ADDRESS], Apartment Number _____, [CITY, STATE ZIP], as is, which [are/are not] heated, for a lease term beginning on _____ [DATE typically 1st of month] and renewing each month thereafter, at a rent as follows:

Each rental period shall consist of one (1) month, lasting from the first day of that month through and including the last day of that month, and renewing each month thereafter. The rental periods shall continue until this agreement either expires or is terminated by either party in accordance with the terms herein.

For each rental period, the rent shall be **$**_____ per month payable on the **first (1ˢᵗ) day of each month in advance**.

Landlord may increase the rent upon 30 days notice to tenant as allowed by [STATE] law.

I could simply add signature lines and conclude the contract here, except that there are many other protective items that should be agreed upon prior to handing over the keys to the tenant, and they are as follows:

Financial Terms

Each of the following terms cover in-depth how rent should be paid, to whom, and when due (item 1). If rent is late (item 2), consequences are indicated. Security and last month rent should be held in an interest-bearing checking account from which tenant should be paid annual interest. It is imperative to check the last month's rent and security deposit laws in your state as that is typically what bad tenants will rely on to "get back at you" should you try to evict them. In some states, violation of these laws will land a tenant a windfall which may exceed the amount of money you are seeking from them. This will result in a very unpleasant court experience for the landlord.

A security deposit should not be returned to the tenant only if there are documented damages to the apartment attributable to tenant or tenant's guest that the tenant has not repaired prior to moving out of the premises. Be sure to keep receipts for products purchased and labor paid as a result of the cost to repair any damages. Security is not required to be refunded less than 30 days from the move-out (according to Massachusetts law). There is also a clause here that indicates a nonrefundable deposit for holding the apartment. The last thing you want to do is spend a couple of thousand dollars to prep an apartment and attain the proper paperwork only to have someone simply pull out of the deal at the eleventh hour leaving your apartment vacant for another month. This will happen.

Following is an example of several lease clauses. These and any other legal language in this book are here for the purposes of example only and cannot be relied upon to be legal in your state. You must review your local laws prior to utilizing any contract language to ensure it complies with your state's laws.

1. **Rent.** Tenant agrees to pay, without demand, to landlord as rent for the demised premises, the sums as explained above each month in advance on the first day of each calendar month beginning _____ [DATE]. Rent shall be paid either in person, if paid in cash to a manager of the LLC, or by check or money order made payable to [LANDLORD], and check or money order may be paid in person to a manager or may be mailed to:

   [ADDRESS TO SEND PAYMENT]

2. **Fees for Late and Non-sufficient Funded Checks.**
   i. Rent not received by the fifth (5th) day of the month will be subject to a $25.00 late fee.
   ii. Any and all charges incurred by landlord as a result of checks being returned for non-sufficient funds (NSF) will be paid by tenant along with a thirty-dollar ($30) fee to cover all penalties. If unpaid, this will be considered a violation of this lease.
   iii. Failure to provide rent on or before the fifth (5th) day of the month will result in eviction.

3. **Security Deposit.** The total security deposit due for the premises is $_____. On execution of this agreement, tenant has deposited $_____ with landlord, receipt of which is hereby acknowledged as deposit toward the full amount stated herein for the faithful performance by tenant of the terms hereof, to be returned to tenant, on the full faithful performance by him of the provisions hereof.

4. **Last Month's Rent.** The total last month's rent due for the premises is $_____. On execution of this agreement, tenant has deposited $_____ with landlord, receipt of which is hereby acknowledged as deposit toward the full amount stated herein.

Any deposit paid to the landlord in order to reserve this apartment is hereby considered nonrefundable and will not be returned in the event tenant decides not to take apartment. Tenant has hereby deposited _____ to hold this apartment.

Tenant understands that tenant will not be allowed to take possession of the premises unless and until the full amount of the security deposit is paid to the landlord. Should tenant fail to pay the full amount of security deposit by the start date of this lease, this lease may be terminated at the sole discretion of the landlord with no recourse available to the tenant.

Remaining Terms

The remaining terms on the lease cover any and all regulations that you have for the tenant. These are all self-explanatory and simply provide reasonable expectations for a safe and habitable environment. In so much as these terms are intended to protect you and all tenants, this is a living situation, and you will need to determine the level of adherence to the lease. For instance, standard to all my leases is a no-smoking clause. Often, I have witnessed individuals smoking in and around apartments. Is this cause for eviction? That would depend upon how strictly one wishes to adhere to the contract. However, it cannot hurt to have many terms at your disposal.

Inspector Syndrome

Despite the benefit of housing assistance programs, they are not without their challenges. Many landlords do not utilize such programs because of the litany of inspectors and ensuing complications due to the overzealous nature of some inspectors. The following is a list of actual items that inspectors have asked me to address:

1. Sterilize a tenant's bath and shower stall due to mildew.
2. Remove plant growth from the front yard.
3. Install railings in a basement bulk head, which had been locked and off-limits to tenants.
4. Repair a mailbox that the tenant continued to break.
5. Replace screens in windows during the winter.
6. Fill in a hole in an adjacent lot for fear of standing water and mosquitoes in the winter.
7. Fix heat when tenant's heat was turned off by the gas company due to nonpayment by the tenant.
8. Fix doorbell.
9. Repair mailbox when tenant continued to pry open the box after continually losing keys.
10. Replace floor because there was a cracked tile.
11. Photograph full dumpster on day of trash pickup and fine landlord $100.
12. Fine landlord for adjacent neighbor's trash that happened to be moved onto landlord's property.

In my experience, most inspectors are nice, hard-working people who are looking out for the needs of the tenant and the state. Furthermore, they are a benefit to the landlord, in that they provide annualized critiques of the apartment interior, exterior, and basement that might otherwise have been overlooked. However, a true concern to the landlord is the zealot inspector who believes it's his calling to proactively reach out to tenants. In one case, I had a bad tenant perpetuate ongoing issues in their apartment. Due to their unsanitary living style and dog which contributed to the unsanitary conditions, they attracted cockroaches. Further, according to their lease, the dog was not even allowed on the premises and in and of itself was a violation of the lease sufficient to support their eviction. This tenant decided he no longer wanted to pay his rent, went directly to the health inspector, and claimed we were not addressing his issues, even though he had never mentioned such issues to us. In spite of numerous reports from independent contractors of work performed on this unit, the inspector decided that we were not addressing the matter and brought a criminal suit against me, not my company, *me*. Upon attending the hearing and presenting all the evidence of work performed, the magistrate indicated that nothing would be filed unless the work was not addressed. Again, much ado about nothing. While there are multiple frivolous and borderline abusive processes of this inspector, to fight such challenges may be overwhelming. However, this serves to illustrate that you, the landlord, must have all documentation and maintenance records to thwart such unscrupulous inspectors and consequent actions.

Some housing inspectors who work for programs such as the local housing authority offering Section 8 assistance will cap off rents within a specified geography. In one such circumstance when I was denied an annual rent increase, I asked the inspector what increase I would be entitled to if I were to install new hardwood floors, new stainless steel appliances, and granite countertops. His response was that such improvements might result in an increase of $50 to $100 per month for work that could cost well over $10,000. It was clear that this inspector was limited to how much he could rent an apartment for in this region.

Rental Increases

In one particular attempt to increase rents at a different property where the apartments were all similar two-bedroom units, the inspector told me that all units had to have consistent rents. When I purchased the property, one unit was renting for $700, two of the units were renting for $800, and the fourth and nicest unit was at $950. When the nicest unit became vacant, I rented it for $1,200. Another unit was turned over with a new Section 8 tenant at $1,100. Being a man of his word, once the leases were up for the additional two Section 8 tenants, the inspector allowed me to increase their rents to $1,100. These tenants did not incur any additional expense, yet I realized a 34% increase in rent. If you happen to find yourself in a situation where your rents have been capped off by a local housing authority, seek out tenants who are using alternative housing authorities or payment assistance programs that might be more flexible with rent and inspection guidelines. A common misconception is that Section 8 is only offered on a per-city basis. Actually, Section 8 and housing assistant programs are plentiful and there are many vouchers that may be transferred throughout the state. In general, assistance programs typically mandate that the landlord not take any additional rent from tenants beyond what is agreed upon by the housing authority. However, I offer the following suggestions: if there is on-site parking, you may opt to charge a parking fee if legal in your state; for those who have animals that are unauthorized, charge a pet fee if legal in your state. Many landlords apply a fee for storage. I do not advocate this practice, as you become responsible for all the belongings you are storing. In the event of a theft, fire, water damage, and other disasters, you will need to compensate the tenant for their loss, which may not be an easy figure to agree on.

Create Good Habits

Once you decide on a tenant, remind them that the rent is due by the first day of each month. I send letters to tenants with self-addressed envelopes as reminders. Whenever collecting, always provide a receipt. Be sure to tell them not to send cash and only send checks or money orders through the mail. If the tenant should miss a payment and not communicate with you, whether or not they did so intentionally, automatically issue an eviction notice. The notice serves three purposes: primarily, it reminds the tenant of the serious nature of their obligation; secondly, this makes the tenant aware that they have violated a term of their lease; and thirdly, by law you cannot evict someone without first providing written notice. In my experience, I always contact the individual to ask what may have happened. If they sincerely have a problem, I will work out a payment plan. If they simply decided not to pay their rent, I will inform them that I will be proceeding with eviction, which in most circumstances is enough to get them on track again. If all else fails, I will proceed with the eviction process.

Bookkeeping

Also, practice good bookkeeping. What this entails is keeping precise balance sheets throughout the year with a running total of debits and credits preferably itemized and allocated. Save all expense receipts, and create rental receipts for all tenants. I keep an online balance sheet, using a spreadsheet, as a further accounting measure. This will provide you with an accurate assessment of deductions that will come in handy at tax time; your accountant will love you. While I used to use excel spreadsheets, I have found that utilizing QuickBooks or another similar software will prove especially useful at tax time. Moreover, depending upon the size of your business or properties, it may make sense to employ a professional bookkeeper. This will be especially vital at tax time.

In the course of a year, there are multiple debits, credits, and associated notes that impact on your property and consequently your profits.

Cash Flow

As human beings, we have the tendency of being lenient on those who experience hardship. Rest assured, everyone has a problem at some point in his or her life; this is a business and must be run as such. Cash flow is the lifeblood of your investment. This, of all things, must be monitored regularly. That means maintaining full occupancy as much as possible. While a 5% vacancy factor is the norm, it is more likely that the vacancy factor will threaten your nest egg. Maintaining occupancy and effective cash flow can be like a balancing act. The pendulum may be easily offset by unexpected expenses. If at all possible, you should maintain backup funds, also called "reserves," to mitigate these circumstances.

Additional Income

T here are many areas of an investment property by which one may increase the income aside from a rent increase. Any of the following items may provide additional income from the property.

Tax Benefits of Investing

Once you own a property, it is recommended that the property be sold no earlier than two years after your purchase date, thereby reducing capital gains tax. There are many people who consistently flip properties and incur huge capital gains taxes. By the time they have finished their projects, their total realized gain is nearly 30% less. Additional tax benefits are found in the ability to take deductions. There are companies that specialize in cost segregation studies to allow for large property owners to more rapidly depreciate their holdings and better leverage their property. You must check your tax laws and regulations for your state. The following information is what I have learned in transacting business in my home state and is in no way tax advice as I am not an expert in this field.

1031 Tax-deferred Exchange

A 1031 tax-deferred exchange, or simply called a 1031, is a great benefit if you would like to defer payment of taxes on a sale of a property. Essentially, you are given 45 days within which to identify another property for purchase, and 180 days to close on such property. The property must be a higher cost than what is being sold, and you are required to pay taxes on the gain that is not used in the transaction. In order to properly execute a 1031, you must involve a title company skilled with these transactions. IMPORTANT: THE PROPERTY MUST BE SOLD TO THE 1031 COMPANY. THIS MAY NOT BE PERFORMED IF NOT PROPERLY DOCUMENTED AND SIGNED OFF BY THE PARTIES. The 1031 company acts as the conduit for holding your funds in escrow for the prescribed period of time for executing the purchase. Additionally, this language must be in your Purchase and Sale Agreement (P&S). The language may be as simple as "The seller will be conducting a 1031 tax-deferred exchange," or "Property will be sold to buyer or assigns." This is something that your commercial realtor or 1031 company can advise on with regard to specific language required.

Employed properly, this tool is invaluable and could be used perpetually from property to property ad infinitum. I am currently in the midst of a 1031 where I have sold my property for $1.5 million and have another property under agreement to purchase for $2.5 million. If I had not conducted the 1031, my $300K in equity would have been reduced to approximately $150K. With my additional $200K, I would only be able to finance a property valued at $175K, 30% less.

There are additional features of the 1031 tax code such as a reverse 1031. With a reverse 1031, you would place the identified property for purchase under agreement prior to selling your property. The reverse 1031 is a more complicated and risky process in that your time frame to perform this transaction is tighter than that of the standard 1031.

Mitigation of Tax

Every year I receive an assessment statement from the city, asking me to fill out rents and other income so that they can tax me more. If their form is not filled out, they will estimate what they believe your income on the property is, and typically do not factor in vacancy. Once the municipal assessor is aware of or perceives that there is an income-generating element of your property, you will be taxed. So it will make most sense for you to fill out the form and return it.

While you may not be able to control what the assessor taps you for, you may be creative in your purchasing practices so as to benefit from the property. For instance, you may *require* the following items for your business in investment property:

1. Car or truck
2. Cell phone(s)
3. Computer
4. Printer/scanner/fax
5. Digital camera—to take pictures of units prior to rental and at varying intervals
6. Video camera—to take video of premises for regular quality assurance
7. Tools and supplies—to take care of and effectively manage your property
8. Property surveys—to evaluate potential investments. You may be interested in investing in Hawaii, Florida, Las Vegas, Europe, Caribbean, etc. A trip to those locations may be required to make that evaluation.

Cell Sites, Billboards, and Profitable Entities

When evaluating property, always be on the lookout for entities such as cell sites, billboards, and other profitable elements. Such entities are the best tenants one can find. They do not talk, smoke, call inspectors, have illegal pets or cause trouble in general; they typically pay more, and their lease terms are substantially longer. I purchased one building which had one cell tower and another one approved for installation. While I might have been content with the monthly rental of these towers, which amounted to approximately $35,000 in annual rent, I was able to sell them for a one-time payout of $440,000, 12.5 times annual rent to a company that purchases cell site leases. There are many companies that do so, and you will need to be prepared to negotiate for the terms that best meet your investment. If your plan is to hold your property long term, you may not wish to sell. However, my motivation for the cell site sale was as follows:

1. Based upon the demographic where I have invested, I typically do not hold a building for longer than five years; twelve-and-half years of income was a windfall.
2. My down payment for this property was $500,000, so the $440,000 represents an 88% return on investment without selling my building; with the sale of the building, if I sell for the same price for which I bought the building, I will have a 200% return. Some may argue that my tax basis will have been reduced as a result of the cell site sale. But this element is contingent upon whether you purchase a building with a cell site or without.
3. From a tax standpoint, I could have conducted a 1031 tax-deferred exchange with the proceeds.
4. The cell sites represent a portion of the building that is of little use and not accessible to anyone else as it is on the roof and in the basement.

Cable and Telephone

With the increasing demands for faster, better cable and affiliated services, many companies will want to sell such services to your tenants. In order to do so, they will need access to your basement to wire the building. These companies make thousands of dollars per year per customer. As a result, it would stand to reason that they should pay you for the right and privilege to wire your building and continue to request access. They will willingly fork over the money for this investment, but you will probably have to *ask* for it. They will not generally offer this to you.

Laundry Machines

Coin-operated laundry machines are a great source of supplemental income. It is important, however, to assess the need and cost of these machines, as well as the environment prior to placing them in your building.

In my experience, coin-operated machines are not beneficial for less than ten units. Even with ten units, you may not see more than a $200 per month return, which you will need to take into account your cost for water and sewer and effectively assess the value of these machines. In addition, you need to consider if the machines will be a temptation for the local vandals and thieves to attempt at getting the coins out of the machines.

There are third party companies that offer programs for machines. They will either maintain or replace the machines you have, pay you money for such machines, and continue to pay you a percentage of the income generated for these machines. This provides a revenue stream that is managed completely by someone else. A nice benefit.

Pet Fees

In subsidized housing scenarios, you are not allowed to collect additional rents from a tenant outside what is contracted in the terms of the rental agreement. However, if the tenant has or desires to have a pet, you may assess a pet fee in some states.

If you opt for a pet fee, you must be careful that this is not abused, or you may end up with mini-zoos in each of your apartments. You must be specific, such as "one Labrador Retriever named Max" or "no more than one cat and one Yorkshire Terrier."

Storage Fees

Space is at a premium. If a tenant would like to store items in your building, you may rent this space, yet it is ill-advised. Insurance companies are always looking for ways to increase your premium or cancel your policy at the first hint of a problem. You may actually lose your insurance if you rent storage areas if not disclosed to the insurance company prior to such rental activity. If there is an issue with the rental areas such as damage to property or personal injury of a tenant, the insurance company may refuse to cover you and you will be left footing the bill which can be very costly. In a more extreme case, you may lose your insurance entirely.

Beware of the liabilities involved with access to these spaces such as potential fire or electric hazards. It should be a safe area devoid of utilities. Never allow storage or placement of flammable or toxic liquids anywhere in the building. Such items to avoid would include gasoline, propane tanks, coal, lighter fluid, kerosene lamps, paint, chemicals, pesticides, gas grills, etc. Also, in order to avoid abuse, you may provide a key or locked facility.

I have some off-street storage containers that may be rented out as well. These are metal containers that are free standing and are in no way attached to, or part of, the building structure.

Parking Fees

Although typically included within the lease, if not stated within the lease, you may opt to rent parking spaces if allowed to do so in your state. Always specify what is available to the tenant or lessee, such as "one parking space for vehicle with license plate number [NUMBER], registered to [NAME]." Do not allow unregistered vehicles to remain on the parking lot. Do not allow anyone to work on vehicles in the parking lot. Post signs that state management is not responsible for property within the parking lot, and that any unauthorized vehicles will be towed at the owner's expense. You should then print and provide parking stickers for the tenants and those paying for parking privileges. Once stickers are issued, contract with a local towing company to monitor the lot and remove any unauthorized vehicles. They typically will not remove unregistered vehicles. Costs of removing vehicles will vary. At my buildings, removal of unregistered unclaimed vehicles may cost $200 per vehicle removed.

Utility and Government Programs

Many utility companies provide programs to assist with reducing energy costs. Such programs may mitigate expenses through a combination of providing free energy efficient appliances and discounts toward purchasing them. For example, my local power company provides such services to its gas and electric customers. In addition, nonprofit and government agencies may provide similar discounts and benefits geared to low-income housing. I benefitted from the removal of an old burner and installation of a $60,000 efficient boiler system as a result of an inquiry to one such agency. This removal and installation cost me absolutely nothing out of pocket.

COVER YOUR ASSETS

Limited Liability Corporation (LLC)

I learned a long time ago to work smarter, not harder. In so doing, this chapter will offer insight into ways in which you might best protect yourself when investing in property. Prior to purchase, and after consulting with a business attorney or doing your own research, establish a shelter such as a Limited Liability Company, a Corporation, a Trust or other vehicle which will suit your purposes. I have chosen to utilize the Limited Liability Company (LLC). I determined based on my situation and goals that, in the early years of property investing, this would provide me with effective coverage. The cost of establishing an LLC in my state is approximately $500 and an Annual Report must be filed each year with the Secretary of State's office. Utilizing this as the vehicle for purchasing the property will provide me some protection from possible lawsuits.

Legal Work and Documentation

Other costs will include that of a good lawyer. In spite of the fact that they are an invaluable resource, many forms used by the attorneys are just forms used by attorneys. Yet the cost for these templates is paid for by you with the attorney's hourly wage and miscellaneous additional costs. There are many sources for already created documentation such as bookstores, Secretary of State offices, online resources, and real estate offices that may supply you with forms specific to your state and region. Once you receive forms such as your first LLC documents, rental agreements, and any other generic agreements, be sure to have copies available so that the next time you are required to use such forms, you may copy from the original templates and save yourself a bundle.

Evictions

The most important element to your investment in rental property is finding good tenants. While it is not an easy task, this will become the most vital element of effectively running your business. One of my most sore topics is that of eviction. It is far less costly to maintain a satisfied tenant than to be rotating tenancy. Unfortunately, eviction is a necessary evil that all landlords must contend with at some time. If you are not prepared to rid yourself of bad tenants, you are destined for failure. Always work toward implementing best practices geared toward effective collection of rents and mitigation of eviction. See Appendix E. There are multiple reasons to evict. Most commonly, evictions are carried out for nonpayment of rent. However, one may serve an eviction for any number of reasons, including but not limited to dealing in drugs, damaging property, threatening the safety of others, and not abiding by any number of lease elements. The following eviction process will provide you with an understanding of the practices enforced in my state. You will need to research local laws governing eviction in your area.

As it stands today, my state provides three separate forms for processing evictions:

1. 48-hour notice to quit for illegal activities occurring within the apartment

2. 14-day notice to quit for nonpayment of rent
3. 30-day notice to quit for eviction without cause in the case of a tenant at will or month-to-month lease term

The 48-hour notice is a rarity. In theory, the time frames represented are reasonable. However, in practice, evicting a tenant in my state takes no less than 46 days with associated costs to the landlord of multiple months of rent, constable fees, court fees, damages to the unit, added utility costs and abuse, additional months of vacancy, occupancy permit, and apartment preparation for future tenants. In the case of a $1,000 rental, it is not uncommon for a landlord to incur $5,000 worth of expenses for a single-unit eviction. Contributing factors to this timely and costly process are the fact that in my state, we have a "traveling court," which meets only on a weekly basis, and not coinciding with the schedule of the eviction can result in an additional time just to appear in front of the housing court. Also, legal holidays such as the Fourth of July, Christmas, etc., can get a tenant an additional week as that holiday may fall on the one weekday that the court is in your jurisdiction. Needless to say, this also causes a backlog of cases to be heard the following week which can result in additional hours being spent in court to be heard. One may pursue an eviction in district court, however such a filing may be removed by the savvy tenant to the Housing Court where they typically deal with such matters in the Commonwealth of Massachusetts. This removal will cause delay in getting your court date.

Stall tactics on the part of a tenant may include frivolous countermeasures in the form of discovery and interrogatories *provided by the courts* to enable the tenant to argue miscellaneous elements of their eviction. Once before the housing clerk, the landlord and tenant must be present. If both parties are present, the parties must appear before a court-appointed mediator. Assuming all items are addressed by the parties and the landlord simply wants the tenant out of the building, the tenant can agree to vacate at any time, however there is a minimum of 10 days provided to the tenant in Massachusetts. Once the 10 days, or days agreed upon by the parties, are up, if the tenant's belongings are still in the apartment, even if you know for a fact that the tenant has abandoned the belongings and the apartment, the landlord must obtain an execution from the court, and is required to have a constable determine if the items in the apartment should be stored and carted away at further expense to the landlord, or if it is all simply junk and can be thrown away. Even that is an additional expense when tenants leave large items such as furniture which you will likely have to pay to have removed and disposed of. Many of the state- and government-supported, low-income-tenant-supported agencies will advocate for the tenant by providing counsel on the eviction process and tenants' rights, along with other tactics to stall an eviction.

There are three general processes for eviction in Massachusetts. They are as follows:

1. 30 day notice to quit for eviction without cause in the case of a tenant at will.
2. 14 day notice to quit for nonpayment of rent in the case of a tenant with any type of tenancy.
3. 48 hour notice to quit in the case of a tenant with any type of tenancy.

Sounds simple, right? Do not be fooled by the names of these processes.

1. In the case of a tenant at will, or a month-to-month tenant, in accordance with Massachusetts General Laws, the landlord need give only 30 days notice to terminate the tenancy, however you must watch the days of the month. If you want to evict someone by the end of July, you must serve them the notice no later than the last day of June. In other words, "30 days" is not just any 30 days. It is a time period in which the 30th day is the final day of the month. Technically you could give someone a 30 day notice on

June 5th, but the "30th" day is still July 31, the last day of the last full month of residency. This 30 day notice is for any reason or no reason at all. It is simply how the tenancy at will operates. Having explained this, why would a tenant need to be heard in court under the terms of a 30 day notice to quit if he is a tenant at will? Claiming defenses such as retaliation or bad apartment conditions should have nothing to do with termination of the tenancy by the landlord, however under Massachusetts General Laws, the tenant may claim these, and other, defenses. If you have bad tenants who are well versed in the eviction process, expect them to raise every defense available to them, whether or not they are true.

2. The 14 day notice is provided to the landlord to expedite the eviction timeframe from a 30 day period in the case of a tenant at will, or from the expiration of a lease term in the case of a tenant with a long term or annual lease. This is to assist the landlord from being financially burdened by a tenant who is not paying rent. Remember, not only are they not paying rent, but in many cases, they are running up your water and sewer bill, your fuel bill and other miscellaneous expenses related to the tenancy. Again, be prepared that the tenant may raise the same defenses and allegations as described above. Nothing is as simple as it should be in the world of a landlord.

3. In the case of a 48 hour notice to quit, there must be illegal activity actually occurring in the apartment. For example, the tenant is selling drugs out of the apartment or there is prostitution occurring in the apartment. To utilize the 48 hour notice, supporting documentation may need to be attached to prove the existence of the illegal activity in the unit. For example, a police report detailing a drug raid on an apartment and resulting arrests. In this case, the landlord should not be burdened further with the threat of continuing illegal activity on his property. Further, *it is fundamentally unfair to the other tenants in the building*

to force them to continue to live in a dangerous situation. Keep in mind however, that if you determine that a career criminal is living in one of your apartments, you simply cannot use the 48 hour notice if he is committing none of that illegal activity at the apartment. At that point, you must resort to a 30 day notice assuming he is a tenant at will.

I will now summarize for you the eviction process using, as an example, a 14 day notice to quit for nonpayment of rent, as I am assuming this is probably the majority of the cases that come before the court with which I take issue. Note that the number of days after day 18 below are estimates since there is a window of time in which you can serve the document and then file it with the court. These numbers assume that the document is filed with the court one week, or 7 days, later.

Day 1 Rent is due.
Day 2 Rent remains unpaid.
Day 3 Service of 14-day notice to quit is served on the tenant. In Massachusetts, a constable is not required at this stage, but to be able to prove service, you may hire one at a cost of $35 to $50, depending on which constable is used. Tenant now has until 14 days later to vacate.
Day 17 Tenant opts to remain in apartment.
Day 18 Tenant is served with Summary Process Summons and Complaint at a cost of $35 to $50, depending on which constable is used. In Massachusetts, this must be served by a constable or sheriff. In addition to the cost of service, in Massachusetts, this document has the Court's raised seal and costs $5 just for the paper. Tenant and landlord now have the following timeline to comply with:
Day 25 (Or the first Monday after service of the summons) Landlord must file the said Summary Process Summons and Complaint with the Housing Court along with a copy of the 14 day notice to quit and the filing fee

charged by the court. In Massachusetts, and at the time of the writing of this book, the fee was $135.00 per apartment.

Day 32 Tenant must file his answer and counterclaim if any. If he files an answer, counterclaim, or serves you with interrogatories (legal questions) and requests for discovery (documentation), the trial date is postponed by two weeks. For the sake of this example, we will assume that no delay has occurred.

Day 39 Trial date is scheduled during this week. Since the Housing Court in Massachusetts travels to different locations, you would need to coordinate your eviction calendar with the dates that the court is in session in the county where you are pursuing the eviction. Due to such availability, this will create further delays. In my situation, our court sessions take place on a Tuesday, so I will use that as a number to continue this example.

Day 40 Trial day begins with mediation. Some courts require that the parties sit with a mediator, while others make it optional. The parties present their case to the court-appointed mediator. This can take place in a private room or, where space is limited, simply standing in the hallway. Generally the parties can come to terms with the mediator. When dealing with low income properties, the tenants have no means of paying past due rent and, truth be told, you just want them out and to regain possession of your apartment. Should you not be able to come to a resolution and you must go before the Judge, the minimum the court will allow the tenant to vacate is 10 days from this trial day. If you are successful in mediation, the parties can agree to less time, but if you have a career bad tenant, this will likely not happen. For purposes of this example, we will assume that the tenant has 10 days to vacate.

Day 50 Tenant has not vacated. Landlord must now snail mail a request to the court for an execution to be served by a constable or sheriff at a much higher cost than service of a simple Summons and Complaint. If you are requesting the execution simply to move a tenant out, you can receive that execution by return snail mail. If you are also seeking to enforce collection of unpaid monies agreed upon on trial day, you must file a Motion to be heard by the Judge and present your argument in person. This requires another day spending your time in court and a number of days before that hearing can be held. Again you are delayed in this process.

Day 55 Assuming two days for the mail to arrive at the clerk's office, one day for the execution to issue, and another two days for the mail to return to you, you should have your execution in hand by day 55. Now you must have it served at a very high cost.

Day 56 The constable or sheriff serve the execution on the tenant giving them notice that they have 48 hours to move out or the constable or sheriff will return with a bonded, licensed eviction moving company to move them out forcibly.

Day 58 Should you be unlucky enough to find yourself still in this process at this time, you will now be paying the constable or sheriff, again, to show up for the actual move out. You must hire and pay special eviction movers at a high cost, and you must pay for a certain amount of storage for their belongings.

Note that if the tenant filed an answer and counterclaims or request for production of documents, he has now delayed the process an additional two weeks not reflected here.

This process for a 14-day notice to quit for nonpayment of January rent has now taken 58 days, assuming an answer was not filed. If an answer and counterclaims had been filed, we would be at day 72, not to mention the extra time a landlord must spend putting together all of the requested documentation and answering the questions posed by the tenant. There are consequences for the landlord should you not comply with this requirement. And one last thought on timing; should a legal holiday fall on the day that is your jurisdiction's trial day, you lose an additional week in Massachusetts. That would make it a grand total of 79 days.

So, finally the landlord successfully evicts the tenant and incurs all expenses of multiple services by constable or sheriff, moving and storage fees, and do not forget, lost rent for 58 to 79 days, all for a tenant who stopped paying rent and was a tenant at will. This is simply abuse of process and fundamentally unfair. Unfortunately, the courts show no signs of changing any time soon.

It is not uncommon for tenants to resort to a number of other tactics to remain in their apartment rent-free. Following their damage to the unit, the tenant will then contact a local board of health or housing agency, decrying their plight. The agency responds by sending full forces of representatives to inspect not simply the apartment but the whole building and surrounding premises to ensure code is maintained. The presence of a mop and bucket in a main hallway would result in a notice stating that all common areas must be clear, and containing threats of meeting the agencies' demands, or else fines will be levied on the landlord. This is a vicious cycle full of tenants with the intent to milk this system. In one recent example, a tenant for whom we provided nine separate documented treatments from an extermination company, continued to claim that they were experiencing issues with bugs and would not be paying their rent. After some further investigation, it became clear that they were experiencing some financial challenges and were simply avoiding paying their rent. Unfortunately, their avoidance and inability to effectively communicate with us resulted in a barrage of calls from city inspectors and agencies that are seemingly in business to promote such activity. With such activity and involvement from these agencies, the tenant becomes emboldened, and will indicate that the eviction is "retaliatory." Massachusetts law protects a tenant from being evicted within six months of making a report against a landlord, or reporting bad conditions to the landlord. Such an eviction would or could be considered "retaliatory". Of course, if you have legitimate ground to evict that tenant, you should proceed. In the example above, the tenant claimed we were retaliating, however we were still able to get them out because we had a legitimate reason to do so.

Beyond the nuisance of coping with this inefficient system is the constant barrage of tools provided to the tenant by the Commonwealth, including free counsel who only result in further expense and frustration to an already ridiculous process. In another step toward enabling tenancy and costing landlords, recently the court passed a rule that requires landlords who own property under a company designation to use an attorney. Looked at another way, this is probably a good thing for the landlord as it ensures that the attorney will likely not miss deadlines or prolong tenancy through mistakes. Evictions are typically the result of a tenant either not paying their rent for a period of time or for some other violation of their agreement. Regardless of the reason, you will be frustrated to comprehend why as an owner of a building, you may not simply remove a "tenant at will" from your premises without such a litany of bureaucracy and expense. This abuse of the system is well portrayed in the film *Pacific Heights*. The way the laws work today, if someone were to simply move into an apartment without the consent of the landlord, even if this person were a "guest" of the tenant, and if that person were to remain in the apartment, the landlord would be required to go through the same eviction process to remove that individual. Instituting more appropriate laws for eviction is more responsible for the health of the community since often times tenants who know how to play the system may continue to abuse the system without concern for any interruption. Unfortunately, many tenants are aware of the advantage they have with manipulating the system. These tenants realize that inherent to the system are these time gaps and loopholes that enable them to simply live free for at least two months, at which point they will move on to the next unsuspecting landlord for another two months. All the while, these individuals are sapping the resources of the Commonwealth, charitable agencies, utility companies, and the landlords. Ultimately, you may be better served to pay the tenant to vacate the apartment and save yourself from the litany of abuse. In one case, I had a tenant who, after being well into the eviction process, began using the apartment to breed pit bulls. I needed to hire a dog officer and prove that the apartment had been vacated, and the officer struggled to remove these vicious dogs. Soon thereafter, these tenants returned to the building when a fire suspiciously occurred, after they had informed other tenants to "watch this." I will discuss this in the Insurance chapter.

In the area where my properties exist, the homeless shelters will not allow an individual to move in unless they can furnish proof of eviction from their apartment. This creates a further burden on the tenant and the landlord to further fuel this inefficient cycle of irresponsibility. At a minimum, the landlord is required to pay a constable or sheriff for service of process, and a filing fee with the court. In Massachusetts, the filing fee in the Housing Court is $135.00 per case as of the date of the writing of this book. All of this to typically recover no money, and help the tenant get into a homeless shelter where the state can support them.

There have been many situations in which a tenant appeals to my goodwill, indicates that they are having a difficult time making payments, and perhaps suggests a payment plan or lesser cost apartment. Each time, I have been left in a situation in which the tenant still cannot afford back payments and inevitably ends up in the same situation requiring an eviction. It never ceases to amaze me how the old adage "No good turn goes unpunished" applies to being a landlord. Do not fall prey to individual hardships. After all, this is a business, you are not a bank, and the mortgage company and utilities still need to be paid. You must never confuse being a landlord with anything other than the business of renting apartments.

Build a Network

Working smarter also entails utilizing your network to the best of your capabilities. Your real estate broker is integral to bringing you quality properties that meet your criteria. Share your objectives with a diligent realtor. If they are responsive and hardworking, you will hear back from them often. If they are not, find another more aggressive one. They should be all about service. After all, you will be providing them with income. It is important to note that you are responsible to make the right decision for your best interest. You must never forget that real estate brokers are ultimately motivated by selling a property, and therefore, their motivation may be at odds with you. I have had brokers attempt to convince me that a property was a good deal since the seller had dropped the price and conceded to certain requests of mine. Unfortunately, the seller did not drop the price to the point where I believed the property would be profitable.

Equally important is the mortgage broker. The good broker will shop the products and terms for you. If you are purchasing properties of four family units and less, your options are greater, and there are more resources including banks. Once you cross the four-family barrier, your options lesson, and you will be in greater reliance upon a creative mortgage broker.

You should become familiar with, and engender yourself to, other landlords and property owners. If there is an association, join it. There are multiple lessons to be learned from those who have experienced the pitfalls and nuances of property management. I have been called, and I continue to call others for advice, industry contacts, and other needs. Moreover, having such a relationship will undoubtedly put you first in line for an older investor who wants to sell his assets.

Insurance

Damage to property following drunk driver hitting building

Insuring an investment property has become increasingly more challenging due to increasing costs of insurance and the decrease in companies providing such insurance to this segment of property. Many insurance companies are not insuring buildings near the ocean due to flooding risks. Insurance companies are in business to make money on calculated risks. If you are unfortunate enough to experience a loss, this will become part of your property "loss runs" or record of insurance claims. Your risk assessment will not be known to you but will be transparent to the insurance company that either underwrites your risk or declines due to your level of perceived risk. If the insurance company declines, you are bound by your mortgage to secure proper insurance to cover your property and will, therefore, be regimented to a subprime insurance company which will charge higher rates. As is the case with any other specialized trade, insurance is an art. Be sure to do business with an experienced agent who may guide you with the most suitable products for your building.

Despite the efforts of these professionals, you may still encounter the wrath of insurance company power. Underwriters of insurance companies may seemingly arbitrarily revoke your policy based upon what they perceive to be threats. I experienced this the hard way. Soon after purchasing a large building with my insurance intact, an inspector paid a visit, and a letter was immediately forwarded to me canceling the policy. Replacement of this policy resulted in an increase of $10,000, double the initial premium. The cancellation was based upon assumptions made by the inspector. In spite of the inaccuracies and fallacious comments made by the inspector, I was not given the opportunity to see the complaint, refute these statements, or make the insurance company aware that the legitimate concerns had already been addressed.

Insurance inspectors, like other types of inspectors, are a varied lot. Some may have power trips, while others are sensible individuals with the intent to simply doing the right thing. I have experienced both. At one of my buildings, one inspector required me to remove a railing, only to be told a few months later that there should be a railing. Part of the confusion arises due to the fact that many of these companies use independent inspectors with differing perspectives. Mutual insurance companies operate with different guidelines than public insurance companies.

Tort Torts

In the practice of law, torts refer to civil wrongs. Unfortunately, we have, in our litigious society, those who will perform unethical acts and those who will support such frivolity in an effort to obtain a monetary settlement. Often an attorney will file suit on behalf of an individual claiming personal injury, banking on the fact that most insurance companies will settle a suit for a significant enough value to justify the action of filing. Whether or not the individual has been harmed is irrelevant, as the attorney will promote this practice, which is commonly referred to as ambulance chasing.

I cannot stress enough the necessity of a good insurance policy. While in process of evicting a tenant and his family for miscellaneous malicious acts, to include drug dealing and lack of payment, the tenant, in a drunken stupor, claimed to have fallen down the staircase and attributed his fall to a broken railing. His carefully orchestrated movements play like a prime-time drama replete with ambulance-chasing attorneys, a trip to the hospital, and trumped-up chiropractic bills. To add insult to injury, he and his ambulance-chasing accomplice determined that his self-directed chiropractic visits amounted to $5,000, while the remainder of his $20,000 claim was attributable to his pain and suffering. In a well-rehearsed delivery, the tenant contacted me to snidely inform me that he would be filing suit against me. Notwithstanding the annoyance of these actions, my deductible, in this case, $2,000, took care of this nuisance. A short time later, another individual surfaced to claim the same thing happened to her nearly one year earlier. In the second situation, the first ambulance chaser declined the case, the second was disbarred, and the third is still fraudulently pursuing this matter. Coincidentally, the second "injured" party was the friend of the first "injured" party.

In yet another example, a disgruntled tenant undergoing an eviction caused a fire in one apartment, resulting in a $130,000 payout by the insurance company. At time of renewal, the insurance company dropped the building and refused to renew the policy due to the previous payout, resulting in a higher premium with a subprime insurer.

Fraud

Fraud occurs in situations where people file fraudulent, or bogus, claims for profitable gains. Be concerned about this. After six years of property investing, this happened to me in one building. A tenant who had been served and well in process of eviction decided it was time to retaliate and allegedly fell down a flight of stairs. Witnesses had claimed that he was inebriated. Despite such assertions and regular inspections by management, building inspectors, housing authorities, and insurance companies, ambulance-chasing attorneys prevail. Insurance companies are extremely profitable entities, which have calculated that mitigation of lengthy trials and potential payouts is worse than simply settling a relatively small claim of tens of thousands of dollars to ambulance chasers and their charlatan minions.

Flood and Sewage

One of the most insidious sources of damage is that of water and sewage. Water is the everlasting erosion element. From an insurance perspective, water will saturate and ruin floors, ceilings, walls, furniture, and belongings, causing thousands of dollars in damage. If moisture permeates the walls of your dwelling, it may result in mold (see Environmental Hazards). Mitigation of disaster is always paramount, but accidents happen. Sewage pipes may burst. Your tenants may dispose of the wrong elements into the system which may create larger issues.

Fire Inspectors

Another vital element to owning property is safety. Always ensure that you are in compliance with the code of the local fire department of the municipality where the building is located. There are many federal and state laws governing adherence to fire code;

however, the local fire department has the authority to govern how the code will be within their region.

Smoke Detectors

There are specific codes that mandate the placement of, and volume of, smoke detectors in your building. Often, depending upon the size of your property, code may dictate having hard-wired smoke detectors. In certain buildings, typically four units or more, you will be required to have a hard-wired system, incorporating a fire box that may contact the local fire department. You may use certified electricians or systems companies skilled with these devices.

Carbon Monoxide (CO)

Massachusetts recently passed Nicole's Law, which was named after a young girl who was a victim of carbon monoxide poisoning. This law requires that all Massachusetts buildings be equipped with carbon monoxide detectors in areas that utilize gas or combustion-emitting carbon monoxide. While the laws are specific as to having these detectors in every unit, there are allowances for large properties to have hard-wired systems in and around the gas utilities and driers if applicable. As previously stated, these laws are specific to the local fire department. Always have the fire department authorize the safety of your system for the benefit and safety of you and your tenants.

Business Acumen

This is your business and hence should be treated as such. Treat your tenants with respect, and they will respect you. Set up a file cabinet with a file for each tenant. Include in this file all correspondence, lease agreement, work receipts, etc. Get a mailbox and a separate telephone number, either a cell phone or an office phone, for all business-related matters. Read up on as much information as you can find via the Internet. In addition to your local online attorneys general office, the following sites may provide some assistance:

http://www.rentlaw.com/

http://www.thelpa.com/lpa/free-forms.html

http://www.uslegalforms.com/landlordtenant/

http://www.nolo.com/resource.cfm/catID/5944A0DA-71B3-49EA-BF5D300558FB66A9/213/178/

Following are forms which are included here for your reference, however you should not rely on them to comply with all laws as each state has its own spin on the law.

With the information provided to you in this book, you should be well armed to jump into the real estate investment property marketplace. Be consistent, plan your work, work your plan, and accumulate your empire.

Good luck!

Michael J. Margolis

Appendix A

Property Performa

Property Name/Address: 6 Family Property at X Street, City, State Zip			
Apartment Breakdown	**Quantity**	**Rent**	**$/Month**
1 BR	2	$ 1,000.00	$ 2,000.00
2 BR	4	$ 1,200.00	$ 4,800.00
Total	6		$ 6,800.00
Income			**$/Year**
Rental	$ 81,600.00		$ 24,000.00
Laundry (2.5/APT/WK)	$ 5,200.00		$ 57,600.00
Vacancy (10%)	$ 8,160.00		$ 81,600.00
Total	**$ 78,640.00**	**Asking price:**	**$599,900.00**
Expenses (add/remove items)		Purchase price	$565,000.00
Oil (converted)	$ 2,400.00	Cap rate	6.42%
Gas (water)	$ 1,800.00	Payment per month	$2,857
Electric	$ 150.00	Payment per year	$34,283
Water and sewer	$ 2,000.00	**Net operating income (NOI)**	$36,292
Maintenance	$ 3,000.00	Times earnings	15.57
Vacancy (5%)	$ 28,250.00	Cost per unit	$ 94,166.67
Insurance	$ 2,615.00	Purchase price	$565,000.00
City Tax	$ 2,133.22	% Down	20.0%
Total	**$ 42,348.22**	Down payment	$113,000.00
Total monthly payment (P&I, taxes and insurance)	$ 5,411.11	Loan amount	$452,000.00

Monthly P&I	$ 2,856.95	Loan term	360
Enter property tax rate	10%	Assumptions	
Assessment (at 70% Mkt. value)	$ 395,500.00	Enter interest rate	6.50%
Annual property taxes	$ 2,400.00	Monthly taxes	$ 200.00
Annual expense/net income	$ 2,008.41	Homeowners insurance/monthly	$ 2,354.17

Appendix A (Continued)

Straight Amortization without Additional Principal Payments

Period	Payment	Principal	Interest	Balance	Equity
1	2,856.95	408.61	2,448.33	451,591.39	113,408.61
2	2,856.95	410.83	2,446.12	451,180.56	113,819.44
3	2,856.95	413.05	2,443.89	450,767.51	114,232.49
4	2,856.95	415.29	2,441.66	450,352.22	114,647.78
5	2,856.95	417.54	2,439.41	449,934.68	115,065.32
6	2,856.95	419.80	2,437.15	449,514.87	115,485.13
7	2,856.95	422.08	2,434.87	449,092.80	115,907.20
8	2,856.95	424.36	2,432.59	448,668.44	116,331.56
9	2,856.95	426.66	2,430.29	448,241.78	116,758.22
10	2,856.95	428.97	2,427.98	447,812.81	117,187.19
11	2,856.95	431.29	2,425.65	447,381.51	117,618.49
12	2,856.95	433.63	2,423.32	446,947.88	118,052.12
13	2,856.95	435.98	2,420.97	446,511.90	118,488.10
14	2,856.95	438.34	2,418.61	446,073.56	118,926.44
15	2,856.95	440.72	2,416.23	445,632.84	119,367.16
16	2,856.95	443.10	2,413.84	445,189.74	119,810.26

APPENDIX B

Month-to-month/Tenant-at-will

RENTAL AGREEMENT—MONTH-TO-MONTH TERM

Date: _____

[LANDLORD NAME AND ADDRESS] rents and the

Tenant: _____   SS# _____

Tenant:_____   SS# _____

hires the premises at [PROPERTY ADDRESS], Apartment Number _____, [CITY, STATE ZIP], as is, which [are/are not] heated, for a lease term beginning on _____ [DATE typically 1st of month] and renewing each month thereafter, at a rent as follows:

- Each rental period shall consist of one (1) month, lasting from the first day of that month through and including the last day of that month, and renewing each month thereafter. The rental periods shall continue until this agreement either expires or is terminated by either party in accordance with the terms herein.

- For each rental period, the rent shall be $_____ per month payable on the **first (1ˢᵗ) day of each month in advance.**
- Landlord may increase the rent upon 30 days' notice to tenant as allowed by [STATE] law.

Unless otherwise specified herein, this tenancy may be terminated only in the form of written 30-day notice given by either party to the other, and shall be effective at the end of the lease term after such notice has been given; provided, however, that in the event of any breach of this agreement by tenant, landlord shall be entitled to pursue any and all remedies provided herein or recognized by applicable law. This tenancy shall be under the following terms and conditions:

1. **Rent.** Tenant agrees to pay, without demand, to landlord as rent for the demised premises, the sums as explained above each month in advance on the **first** day of each calendar month beginning _____ 1, 2007. **Rent shall be paid by check or money order made payable to [LANDLORD/MANAGER], and check or money order must be sent to:**

   [ADDRESS FOR PAYMENT]

2. **Fees for Late and Non-sufficient Funded Checks.**
   i. Rent not received by the fifth (5ᵗʰ) day of the month will be subject to a $25.00 late fee.
   ii. Any and all charges incurred by landlord as a result of checks being returned for non-sufficient funds (NSF) will be paid by tenant along with a thirty-dollar ($30) fee to cover all penalties. If unpaid, this will be considered a violation of this lease.
   iii. Failure to provide rent on or before the fifth (5ᵗʰ) day of the month will result in eviction.

3. **Security Deposit.** The total security deposit due for the premises is $_____. On execution of this agreement, tenant has deposited $_____ with landlord, receipt of which is hereby acknowledged as deposit toward the full amount stated herein for the faithful performance by tenant of the terms hereof, to be returned to tenant, on the full faithful performance by him of the provisions hereof.

4. **Last Month's Rent.** The total last month's rent due for the premises is $_____. On execution of this agreement, tenant has deposited $_____ with landlord, receipt of which is hereby acknowledged as deposit toward the full amount stated herein.

Any deposit paid to the landlord in order to reserve this apartment is hereby considered nonrefundable and will not be returned in the event tenant decides not to take apartment. Tenant has hereby deposited _____ to hold this apartment.

Tenant understands that tenant will not be allowed to take possession of the premises unless and until the full amount of the security deposit is paid to the landlord. Should tenant fail to pay the full amount of security deposit by the start date of this lease, this lease may be terminated at the sole discretion of the landlord with no recourse available to the tenant.

5. **Quiet Enjoyment.** Tenant covenants that on paying the rent and performing the covenants herein contained, Tenant shall peacefully and quietly have, hold, and enjoy the demised premises for the agreed term.

6. **Use of Premises.** The demised premises shall be used and occupied by tenant exclusively as a private single family residence, and neither the premises nor any part thereof shall be used at any time during the term of this lease by tenant for the purpose of carrying on business, profession,

or trade of any kind, or for any purpose other than as a private single family residence. Tenant shall comply with all the sanitary laws, ordinances, rules, and orders of appropriate governmental authorities affecting the cleanliness, occupancy, and preservation of the demised premises, and the sidewalks connected thereto, during the term of this agreement.

7. **Number of Occupants.** Tenant stipulates that the demised premises shall be occupied by no more than _____ persons, consisting of _____ adult(s) and _____ child(ren), without the written consent of landlord.

8. **Condition of Premises.** Tenant stipulates that he or she has examined the demised premises, including the grounds and all buildings and improvements, and that they are at the time of this agreement, in good order and repair and in safe, clean, and tenantable condition.

9. **Re-keying/Change of Locks.** Any and all re-keying or change of locks to an apartment must be approved by property management and will be subject to a $75.00 fee.

10. **Assignment and Subletting.** Without the prior written consent of landlord, tenant shall not assign this lease or sublet or grant any concession or license to use the premises or any part thereof. Consent by landlord to one assignment, subletting, concession, or license shall not be deemed to be consent to any subsequent assignment, subletting, concession, or license. An assignment, subletting, concession, or license without the prior written consent of landlord, or an assignment or subletting by operation of law, shall be void and shall, at landlord's option, terminate this rental agreement.

11. **Alterations and Improvements.** Tenant shall make no alterations to the buildings on the demised premises or construct any building or make other improvements on the demised premises without the prior written consent of landlord. All alterations, changes, and improvements built,

constructed, or placed on the demised premises by tenant, with the exception of fixtures removable without damage to the premises and moveable personal property, shall, unless otherwise provided by written agreement between landlord and tenant, be the property of landlord and remain on the demised premises at the expiration or sooner termination of this rental agreement.

12. **Damage to Premises.** If the demised premises, or any part thereof, shall be partially damaged by fire or other casualty not due to tenant's negligence or willful act or that of his employee, family, agent, or visitor, the premises shall be promptly repaired by landlord; but if the premises should be damaged due to tenant's negligence or willful act or that of his employee, family, agent, or visitor to the extent that landlord shall decide to rebuild or repair, the tenant shall be fully liable for all costs and expenses directly or indirectly related to rebuilding and repair of same. Tenant's security deposit, at the option of landlord, can be used to pay for some or all of said rebuilding and repair. In the event that rebuilding and repair exceeds the amount of the security deposit on account, tenant shall be responsible for paying landlord the excess amount within 30 days of notification of the actual cost of the rebuilding or repairs.

13. **Dangerous Material.** Tenant shall not keep or have on the premises any article or thing of a dangerous, flammable, or explosive nature that might unreasonably increase the danger of fire on the premises or that might be considered hazardous or extra hazardous by any responsible insurance company.

14. **Utilities.** Tenant shall be responsible for arranging for and paying for all utility services required on the premises, except that water and sewage shall be provided by landlord.

15. **Right of Inspection:** Landlord and their agents shall have the right at all reasonable times during the term of this rental agreement and any renewal thereof to enter the demised premises for various purposes including but not limited to that of inspecting the premises, performing

repairs and conducting general maintenance. Inspection of premises will be performed at least once a year.

16. **Maintenance and Repair.** Tenant will, at his or her sole expense, keep and maintain the demised premises and appurtenances in good sanitary condition and repair during the term of this lease and any renewal thereof. In particular, tenant shall keep the fixtures in the house or on or about the demised premises in good order and repair; keep the furnace clean; keep the electric bills in order; keep the walks free from dirt, snow and debris; take out the trash; and, at his or her sole expense, make all required repairs to the plumbing, oven and stove, heating apparatus, and electric and gas fixtures whenever damage thereto shall have resulted from tenant misuse, waste, or neglect or that of his employee, family, agent, or visitor. Tenant agrees that no trash will be left in the main hallways or areas of building. Tenant agrees that no signs shall be placed or painting done on or about the demised premises by tenant or at his direction without the prior written consent of landlord.

17. **Animals. Tenant shall keep no domestic or other animals on or about the demised premises without the written consent of landlord.**

18. **Display of Signs and Re-rental.** During the last 30 days of this rental agreement, landlord or their agent shall have the privilege of displaying the usual "FOR SALE" or "FOR RENT" signs on the demised premises and of showing the property to prospective purchasers or tenants. Upon 12 hours' notice, landlord shall have permission to show the apartment to prospective new tenants.

19. **Surrender of Premises.** This agreement shall be terminated on 30 days' written notice served by either the landlord or the tenant. At this time, the tenant should quit and surrender the premises hereby demised in as good a state and condition as they were at the time of occupancy. Reasonable use and wear thereof and damages by the elements shall be excepted from this provision.

20. Default. If any default is made in the payment of rent, or any part thereof, at the times hereinbefore specified, or if any default is made in the performance of or compliance with any other term or condition hereof, the rental agreement, at the option of landlord, shall terminate and be forfeited, and landlord may evict the tenant, reenter the premises, and remove all persons therefrom. Tenant shall be given written notice of any default or breach, and termination and forfeiture of the lease shall not result if, within 10 days of receipt of such notice, tenant has corrected the default or breach or has taken action reasonably likely to effect such correction within a reasonable time, but in any event not longer than an additional 30 days.

21. Abandonment. If at any time during the term of this rental agreement, tenant abandons the demised premises or any part thereof, landlord may, at their option, enter the demised premises by any means without being liable for any prosecution therefore, and without becoming liable to tenant for damages or for any payment of any kind whatever, and may, at their discretion, as agent for tenant, re-let the demised premises, or any part thereof, for the whole or any part of the then unexpired term, and may receive and collect all rent payable by virtue of such re-letting, and at landlord's option, hold tenant liable for any difference between the rent that would have been payable under this rental agreement during the balance of the unexpired term, if this rental agreement had continued in force, and the rent for such period realized by landlord by means of such re-letting. If landlord's right of reentry is exercised, following abandonment of the premises by tenant, then landlord may consider any personal property belonging to tenant and left on the premises to also have been abandoned, in which case landlord may dispose of said personal property in any manner in which landlord shall deem proper and is hereby relieved of all liability for doing so. Landlord may apply any and all remaining security deposit toward repairs and replenishing of apartment.

22. **Binding Effect.** The covenants and conditions herein contained shall apply to and bind the heirs, legal representatives, and assigns of the parties hereto, and all covenants are to be construed as conditions of the rental lease agreement.

23. **Automobile Repairs.** Automobile repairs are absolutely prohibited in any part of the rented property including backyard, parking lot, and driveway.

24. **Trash Removal.** Tenants are responsible for taking out their own trash.

25. **Snow Removal.** Tenants are responsible for clearing snow and ice off their walkways and parking spaces without interfering with other tenants' walkways or parking spaces.

26. **Clear and Clean Passage.** Front porches and all stairwells are to be kept clear of all garbage and debris at all times.

27. **No Smoking.** Smoking is not allowed anywhere on the premises, including hallways, porches, basements, and front and backyards and driveways.

28. **Criminal Acts.** Tenants shall not participate in, or be convicted of, a crime during the term of this agreement.

29. **Drug Use.** Tenants shall not engage in any drug use or other illegal activity on the premises.

30. **Unauthorized Areas.** Under no circumstances shall tenant be allowed in the basement area of the premises, the roof area, the attic area, or any other area other than the common areas used for access to the apartments and the apartments themselves.

31. **Hold Harmless.** Tenant shall hold landlord harmless for any acts of others which cause harm or damage to themselves, their guests, or property.

32. **Legal Fees.** In the event the tenant shall pursue action in a court of law and not prevail, the landlord shall be paid any and all legal fees incurred by landlord.

33. **Lead Paint.** Tenant acknowledges that there is no lead paint in their unit or common areas.

34. **WASHERS AND DRYERS ARE NOT ALLOWED ON THE PREMISES.**

35. **Passageways and Exterior Areas.** No items are to be left in the hallways, stairways, foyers, parking lot, yard areas, or any other areas. Any items left in these areas, including the areas outside of tenant's front and back doors, will be thrown away. If the item is large and there is a charge incurred for removal and disposal of said item, tenant will be charged a removal fee and will pay such fee within 14 days.

36. **ANY FINES CHARGED TO THE LANDLORD BY THE CITY DUE TO THE ACTIONS OF THE TENANT WILL BE CHARGED TO THE TENANT AND THE TENANT WILL PAY THOSE CHARGES WITHIN 14 DAYS.** Example: items left in the hallways causing a fire hazard, etc.

IN WITNESS WHEREOF, the parties have executed this agreement the day and year first above written.

_____

, Tenant

_____

, Manager

[LANDLORD]

NOTICE: State law establishes rights and obligations for parties to rental agreements. This agreement is required to comply with the Truth in Renting Act or the applicable Landlord-Tenant Statute or code of your state. If you have a question about interpretation or legality of a provision of this agreement, you may want to seek assistance from a lawyer or other qualified person.

APPENDIX C

One-year Lease

RENTAL AGREEMENT—ONE-YEAR TERM

Date: _____

[LANDLORD AND ADDRESS] rents and the below named tenant(s)

Tenant: _____ SS# _____

Tenant:_____ SS# _____

hires the premises at [ADDRESS], Apartment Number _____, [CITY, STATE ZIP], as is, consisting of _____ rooms, including _____ bedrooms which are not heated for a lease term beginning on _____ [DATE typically 1st of month] and ending one year thereafter, at a rent as follows:

- Each rental period shall consist of one (1) month, lasting from the first day of that month through and including the last day of that month. The rental periods shall continue until this agreement either expires or is terminated by either party in accordance with the terms herein.
- For each rental period, the rent shall be $_____ per month payable on the first (1st) day of each month in advance.

Unless otherwise specified herein, this tenancy may be terminated only in the form of written notice given by either party to the other, and shall be effective at the end of the lease term after such notice has been given; provided, however, that in the event of any breach of this agreement by tenant, landlord shall be entitled to pursue any and all remedies provided herein or recognized by applicable law. This tenancy shall be under the following terms and conditions:

5. **Rent**. Tenant agrees to pay, without demand, to landlord as rent for the demised premises, the sums as explained above each month in advance on the first day of each calendar month beginning _____[DATE]. Rent shall be paid either in person, if paid in cash to a Manager of the LLC, or by check or money order made payable to [LANDLORD], and check or money order may be paid in person to a manager or may be mailed to:

[ADDRESS TO SEND PAYMENT]

6. **Fees for Late and Non-sufficient Funded Checks.**
    i. Rent not received by the fifth (5th) day of the month will be subject to a $25.00 late fee.
    ii. Any and all charges incurred by landlord as a result of checks being returned for non-sufficient funds (NSF) will be paid by tenant along with a thirty-dollar ($30) fee to cover all penalties. If unpaid, this will be considered a violation of this lease.
    iii. Failure to provide rent on or before the fifth (5th) day of the month will result in eviction.
7. **Security Deposit**. The total security deposit due for the premises is $_____. On execution of this agreement, tenant has deposited $_____ with landlord, receipt of which is hereby acknowledged as deposit toward the full amount stated herein for the faithful performance by tenant of the terms hereof, to be returned to tenant,

on the full faithful performance by him of the provisions hereof.

8. **Last Month's Rent.** The total last month's rent due for the premises is $_____. On execution of this agreement, tenant has deposited $_____ with landlord, receipt of which is hereby acknowledged as deposit toward the full amount stated herein.

Any deposit paid to the landlord in order to reserve this apartment is hereby considered nonrefundable and will not be returned in the event tenant decides not to take apartment. Tenant has hereby deposited _____ to hold this apartment.

9. **Quiet Enjoyment.** Tenant covenants that on paying the rent and performing the covenants herein contained, tenant shall peacefully and quietly have, hold, and enjoy the demised premises for the agreed term.

10. **Use of Premises.** The demised premises shall be used and occupied by tenant exclusively as a private single family residence, and neither the premises nor any part thereof shall be used at any time during the term of this lease by tenant for the purpose of carrying on business, profession, or trade of any kind, or for any purpose other than as a private single-family residence. Tenant shall comply with all the sanitary laws, ordinances, rules, and orders of appropriate governmental authorities affecting the cleanliness, occupancy, and preservation of the demised premises, and the sidewalks connected thereto, during the term of this agreement.

11. **Number of Occupants.** Tenant stipulates that the demised premises shall be occupied by no more than _____ persons, consisting of _____ adult(s) and _____ child(ren) without the written consent of landlord.

12. **Condition of Premises.** Tenant stipulates that he or she has examined the demised premises, including the grounds and all buildings and improvements, and that they are at

the time of this agreement, in good order and repair and in safe, clean, and tenantable condition.

13. **Assignment and Subletting.** Without the prior written consent of landlord, tenant shall not assign this lease, or sublet or grant any concession or license to use the premises or any part thereof. Consent by landlord to one assignment, subletting, concession, or license shall not be deemed to be consent to any subsequent assignment, subletting, concession, or license. An assignment, subletting, concession, or license without the prior written consent of landlord, or an assignment or subletting by operation of law, shall be void and shall, at landlord's option, terminate this rental agreement.

14. **Alterations and Improvements.** Tenant shall make no alterations to the buildings on the demised premises or construct any building or make other improvements on the demised premises without the prior written consent of landlord. All alterations, changes, and improvements built, constructed, or placed on the demised premises by tenant, with the exception of fixtures removable without damage to the premises and moveable personal property, shall, unless otherwise provided by written agreement between landlord and tenant, be the property of landlord and remain on the demised premises at the expiration or sooner termination of this rental agreement.

15. **Damage to Premises.** If the demised premises, or any part thereof, shall be partially damaged by fire or other casualty not due to tenant's negligence or willful act or that of his employee, family, agent, or visitor, the premises shall be promptly repaired by landlord; but if the premises should be damaged due to tenant's negligence or willful act or that of his employee, family, agent or visitor to the extent that landlord shall decide to rebuild or repair, the tenant shall be fully liable for all costs and expenses directly or indirectly related to rebuilding and repair of same. Tenant's security deposit, at the option of landlord, can be used to

pay for some or all of said rebuilding and repair. In the event that rebuilding and repair exceeds the amount of the security deposit on account, tenant shall be responsible for paying landlord the excess amount within 30 days of notification of the actual cost of the rebuilding or repairs.

16. **Dangerous Material.** Tenant shall not keep or have on the premises any article or thing of a dangerous, flammable, or explosive nature that might unreasonably increase the danger of fire on the premises or that might be considered hazardous or extra hazardous by any responsible insurance company.

17. **Utilities.** Tenant shall be responsible for arranging for and paying for all utility services required on the premises, except that water and sewage shall be provided by landlord.

18. **Right of Inspection:** Landlord and their agents shall have the right at all reasonable times during the term of this rental agreement and any renewal thereof to enter the demised premises for various purposes including but not limited to that of inspecting the premises, performing repairs and conducting general maintenance. Inspection of premises will be performed at least once a year.

19. **Maintenance and Repair.** Tenant will, at his or her sole expense, keep and maintain the demised premises and appurtenances in good sanitary condition and repair during the term of this lease and any renewal thereof. In particular, tenant shall keep the fixtures in the house or on or about the demised premises in good order and repair; keep the furnace clean; keep the electric bells in order; keep the walks free from dirt, snow and debris; take out the trash; and, at his or her sole expense, make all required repairs to the plumbing, oven and stove, heating apparatus, and electric and gas fixtures whenever damage thereto shall have resulted from tenant misuse, waste, or neglect or that of his employee, family, agent, or visitor. Tenant agrees that no signs shall be placed or painting done on or about the

demised premises by tenant or at his direction without the prior written consent of landlord.

20. **Animals.** Tenant shall keep no domestic or other animals on or about the demised premises without the written consent of landlord.

21. **Display of Signs and Re-renting.** During the last 30 days of this rental agreement, landlord or their agent shall have the privilege of displaying the usual "FOR SALE" or "FOR RENT" signs on the demised premises and of showing the property to prospective purchasers or tenants. Upon 12 hours' notice, landlord shall have the right to enter to show the apartment to prospective tenants.

22. **Surrender of Premises.** This agreement shall be terminated on 30 days' written notice served by either the landlord or the tenant. At this time, the tenant should quit and surrender the premises hereby demised in as good a state and condition as they were at the time of occupancy. Reasonable use and wear thereof and damages by the elements shall be excepted from this provision.

23. **Default.** If any default is made in the payment of rent, or any part thereof, at the times hereinbefore specified, or if any default is made in the performance of or compliance with any other term or condition hereof, the rental agreement, at the option of landlord, shall terminate and be forfeited, and landlord may evict the tenant, reenter the premises and remove all persons therefrom. Tenant shall be given written notice of any default or breach, and termination and forfeiture of the lease shall not result if, within 10 days of receipt of such notice, tenant has corrected the default or breach or has taken action reasonably likely to effect such correction within a reasonable time, but in any event not longer than an additional 30 days.

24. **Abandonment.** If at any time during the term of this rental agreement, tenant abandons the demised premises or any part thereof, landlord may, at their option, enter the demised premises by any means without being liable for any

prosecution therefor, and without becoming liable to tenant for damages or for any payment of any kind whatever, and may, at their discretion, as agent for tenant, re-let the demised premises, or any part thereof, for the whole or any part of the then unexpired term, and may receive and collect all rent payable by virtue of such re-letting, and at landlord's option, hold tenant liable for any difference between the rent that would have been payable under this rental agreement during the balance of the unexpired term, if this rental agreement had continued in force, and the rent for such period realized by landlord by means of such re-letting. If landlord's right of reentry is exercised following abandonment of the premises by tenant, then landlord may consider any personal property belonging to tenant and left on the premises to also have been abandoned, in which case landlord may dispose of said personal property in any manner in which landlord shall deem proper and is hereby relieved of all liability for doing so.

25. **Binding Effect.** The covenants and conditions herein contained shall apply to and bind the heirs, legal representatives, and assigns of the parties hereto, and all covenants are to be construed as conditions of the rental lease agreement.

26. **Automobile Repairs.** Automobile repairs are absolutely prohibited in any part of the rented property including backyard and driveway.

27. **Trash Removal.** Tenants are responsible for taking out their own trash.

28. **Snow Removal.** Tenants are responsible for clearing snow and ice off their walkways and parking spaces without interfering with other tenants' walkways or parking spaces.

29. **Clear and Clean Passage.** Front porches and all stairwells are to be kept clear of all garbage and debris at all times.

30. **No Smoking.** Smoking is not allowed anywhere on the premises, including hallways, porches, basements and front and backyards, and driveways.

31. **Criminal Acts.** Tenants shall not participate in, or be convicted of, a crime during the term of this agreement.

32. **Drug Use.** Tenants shall not engage in any drug use or other illegal activity on the premises.

33. **Unauthorized Areas.** Under no circumstances shall tenant be allowed in the basement area of the premises, the roof area, the attic area, or any other area other than the common areas used for access to the apartments and the apartments themselves.

34. **Hold Harmless.** Tenant shall hold landlord harmless for any acts of others which cause harm or damage to themselves, their guests, or property.

35. **Legal Fees.** In the event the tenant shall pursue action in a court of law and not prevail, the landlord shall be paid any and all legal fees incurred by landlord.

36. **Lead Paint.** Tenant acknowledges that there is no lead paint in there unit or common areas.

37. **WASHERS AND DRYERS ARE NOT ALLOWED ON THE PREMISES.**

38. **Passageways and Exterior Areas.** No items are to be left in the hallways, stairways, foyers, parking lot, yard areas, or any other areas. Any items left in these areas, including the areas outside of tenant's front and back doors, will be thrown away. If the item is large and there is a charge incurred for removal and disposal of said item, tenant will be charged a removal fee and will pay such fee within 14 days.

39. **ANY FINES CHARGED TO THE LANDLORD BY THE CITY DUE TO THE ACTIONS OF THE TENANT WILL BE CHARGED TO THE TENANT AND THE TENANT WILL PAY THOSE CHARGES WITHIN 14 DAYS.** Example: items left in the hallways causing a fire hazard, etc.

IN WITNESS WHEREOF, the parties have executed this agreement the day and year first above written.

_____   _____
, Tenant   [LANDLORD], Manager

NOTICE: State law establishes rights and obligations for parties to rental agreements. This agreement is required to comply with the Truth in Renting Act or the applicable Landlord-Tenant Statute or code of your state. If you have a question about interpretation or legality of a provision of this agreement, you may want to seek assistance from a lawyer or other qualified person.

APPENDIX D

P&S

PURCHASE AND SALE AGREEMENT

This [DAY#] day of [MONTH, YEAR]

1. Parties and Mailing Addresses

[SELLER NAME], or current owner of premises hereinafter called the SELLER, agrees to SELL and

[BUYER NAME], hereinafter called the BUYER or PURCHASER, agrees to BUY, upon the terms hereinafter set forth, the following described premises:

2. Description

A certain parcel of land with the buildings thereon known as and numbered [ADDRESS AS DESCRIBED IN COUNTY REGISTRY OF DEEDS]; and as more particularly described in a deed recorded at [SPECIFIC REGISTRY] Registry of Deeds in Book [BOOK #] Page [PAGE #]

3. Buildings, Structures, Improvements, Fixtures

Included, in the sale as part of said premises are the buildings, structures, and improvements now thereon, and the fixtures belonging to the SELLER and used in connection therewith including, if any, all wall-to-wall carpeting, drapery rods, automatic garage door openers, venetian blinds, window shades, screens, screen doors, storm windows and doors, awnings, shutters, furnaces, heaters, heating equipment, stoves, ranges, oil and gas burners and fixtures appurtenance thereto, hot water heaters, plumbing and bathroom fixtures, garbage disposers, electric and other lighting fixtures, mantels, outside television antennas, fences, gates, trees, shrubs, plants, and seller-owned refrigerators, washing machines, and dryers.

4. Title Deed

Said premises are to be conveyed by a good and sufficient quitclaim deed running to the BUYER, or to the nominee designated by the BUYER by written notice to the SELLER at least seven days before the deed is to be delivered as herein provided, and said deed shall convey a good and clear record and marketable title thereto, free from encumbrances, except the following:

(a) Provisions of existing building and zoning laws
(b) Existing rights and obligations in party walls which are not the subject of written agreement
(c) Such taxes for the then current year as are not due and payable on the date of the delivery of such deed
(d) Any liens for municipal betterments assessed after the date of this agreement
(e) Easements, restrictions, and reservations of record, if any, so long as the same do not prohibit or materially interfere with the current use of said premises

5. Plans

If said deed refers to a plan necessary to be recorded therewith, the SELLER shall deliver such plan with the deed in form adequate for recording or registration.

6. Registered Title

In addition to the foregoing, if the title to said premises is registered, said deed shall be in form sufficient to entitle the BUYER to a Certificate of Title of said premises, and the SELLER shall deliver with said deed all instruments, if any, necessary to enable the BUYER to obtain such Certificate of Title.

7. Purchase Price

The agreed purchase price for said premises is [SPECIFIC VALUE] dollars and 00/100.

8. Time for Performance: Delivery of Deed

Such deed is to be delivered at [DATE AND TIME], at the [AGREED-UPON LOCATION—typically Registry or the closing attorney's office], unless otherwise agreed upon in writing. It is agreed that time is of the essence of this agreement.

9. Possession and Condition of Premises

Full possession of said premises with all tenants and occupants as described herein is to be delivered at the time of the delivery of the deed, said premises to be then (a) in the same condition as they now are, reasonable use and wear thereof excepted, (b) not in violation of said building and zoning laws, and (c) in compliance with provisions of any instrument referred to in clause 4 hereof. The BUYER shall be entitled personally to inspect said premises prior to the delivery of the deed in order to determine whether the condition hereof complies with the terms of this clause.

The premises are to be delivered in broom clean condition, free of all debris and personal property except for tenant-occupied units.

10. Extension to Perfect Title or Make Premises Conform

If the SELLER shall be unable to give title or to make conveyance, or to deliver possession of the premises, all as herein stipulated, or if at the time of the delivery of the deed the premises do not conform with the provisions hereof, then the SELLER shall use reasonable efforts to remove any defects in title, or to deliver possession as provided herein, or to make the said premises conform to the provisions hereof, as the case may be, in which event the SELLER shall give written notice thereof to the BUYER at or before the time for performance hereunder, and thereupon the time of performance hereof shall be extended for a period of up to thirty days subject to an equal extension to BUYER loan commitment if necessary.

11. Failure to Perfect Title or Make Premises Conform, etc.

If at the expiration of the extended time the SELLER shall have failed so to remove any defects in title, deliver possession, or make the premises conform, as the case may be, all as herein agreed, or if at any time during the period of this agreement or any extension thereof, the holder of a mortgage on said premises shall refuse to permit the insurance proceeds, if any, to be used for such purposes, then any payments made under this agreement shall be forthwith refunded and all other obligations of the parties hereto shall cease and this agreement shall be void without recourse to the parties hereto.

12. Buyer's Election to Accept Title

The BUYER shall have the election, at either the original or any extended time for performance, to accept such title as the SELLER can deliver to the said premises in their then condition and to pay therefore the purchase price without deduction, in which case the SELLER shall convey such title, except that in the event of such conveyance in accord with the provisions of this clause, if the said premises shall have been damaged by fire or casualty insured against, then the SELLER shall, unless the SELLER has previously restored the premises to their former condition, either (a) pay over or assign to the BUYER, on delivery of the deed, all amounts recovered or recoverable on account of such insurance, less any amounts reasonably expended by the SELLER for any partial restoration, or (b) if a holder of a mortgage on said premises shall not permit the insurance proceeds or a part thereof to be used to restore the said premises to their former condition or to be so paid over or assigned, give to the BUYER a credit against the purchase price, on delivery of the deed, equal to said amounts so recovered or recoverable and retained by the holder of the said mortgage less any amounts reasonable expended by the SELLER for any partial restoration.

13. Acceptance of Deed

The acceptance of a deed by the BUYER or his nominee as the case may be, shall be deemed to be a full performance and discharge of every agreement and obligation herein contained or expressed, except such as are, by the terms hereof, to be performed after the delivery of said deed.

14. Use of Money to Clear Title

To enable the SELLER to make conveyance as herein provided, the SELLER may, at the time of delivery of the deed, use the purchase money or any portion thereof to clear the title of any or all encumbrances or interests, provided that all instruments so procured are recorded simultaneously with the delivery of said deed or otherwise in accordance with local conveyancing practice.

15. Insurance

Until the delivery of the deed, the SELLER shall maintain insurance on said premises as follows:

Type of Insurance   Amount of Coverage

(a) Fire and Extended Coverage *$ as presently insured

All risk of loss to remain with SELLER

16. Adjustments

Water use charges, and taxes for the then current fiscal year, shall be apportioned and fuel value shall be adjusted, as of the day of performance of this agreement and the net amount thereof shall be added to or deducted from, as the case may be, the purchase price payable by the BUYER at the time of delivery of the deed, and all leases assigned to BUYER.

17. Adjustment of Unassessed and Abated Taxes

If the amount of said taxes is not known at the time of the delivery of the deed, they shall be apportioned on the basis of the taxes assessed for the preceding fiscal year, with a reapportionment as soon as the new tax rate and valuation can be ascertained; and, if the taxes which are to be apportioned shall thereafter be reduced by abatement, the amount of such abatement, less the reasonable cost of obtaining the same, shall be apportioned between the parties, provided that neither party shall be obligated to institute or prosecute proceeding for an abatement unless herein otherwise agreed.

18. Deposit

All deposits made hereunder shall be held in an interest bearing escrow by Dane, Brady & Haydon, as escrow agent subject to the terms of this agreement and shall be duly accounted for at the time for performance of this agreement. In the event of any disagreement between the parties, the escrow agent shall retain all deposits made under this agreement pending instructions mutually given in writing by the SELLER and the BUYER. Interest shall be paid to BUYER at time of closing and in case of breach of this agreement, the interest will follow the deposit.

19. Buyer's Default Damages

If the BUYER shall fail to fulfill the BUYER's agreements herein, all deposits made hereunder by the BUYER shall be retained by the SELLER as liquidated damages as SELLER'S sole and exclusive remedy at law and in equity.

20. Release by Husband or Wife

The SELLER'S spouse hereby agrees to join in said deed and to release and convey all statutory and other rights and interests in said premises.

21. Broker as Party deleted [MAY BE INSERTED IF BROKER INVOLVED]
22. Liability of Trustee, Shareholder, Beneficiary, etc.

If the SELLER or BUYER executed this agreement in a representative or fiduciary capacity, only the principal or the estate represented shall be bound, and neither the SELLER or BUYER so executing, nor any shareholder or beneficiary of any trust, shall be personally liable for any obligation, express or implied, hereunder.

23. Warranties and Representations

The BUYER acknowledges that the BUYER has not been influenced to enter into this transaction nor has he relied upon any warranties or representations not set forth or incorporated in this agreement or previously made in writing, except for the following additional warranties and representations, if any, made by either the SELLER or the Broker(s): None

24. Mortgage Contingency Clause

In order to help finance the acquisition of said premises, the BUYER shall apply for a conventional bank or other institutional mortgage loan of a minimum of 75% of purchase price at prevailing rates, terms, and conditions. If despite the BUYER's diligent efforts, a written commitment for such loan cannot be obtained on or before January 15, 2008, the BUYER may terminate this agreement by written notice to the SELLER, prior to the expiration of such time, whereupon any payments made under this agreement shall be forthwith refunded and all other obligations of the parties hereto shall cease and this agreement shall be void without recourse to the parties hereto. In no event will the BUYER be deemed to have used diligent efforts to obtain such commitment unless the BUYER submits a complete mortgage loan application conforming to the foregoing provisions to one lender only on or before three days from execution of this agreement.

25. Construction of Agreement

This instrument, executed in multiple counterparts, is to be construed as a Massachusetts contract, is to take effect as a sealed instrument, sets forth the entire contract between the parties, is binding upon and enures to the benefit of the parties hereto and their respective heirs, devisees, executors, administrators, successors, and assigns, and may be canceled, modified, or amended only by a written instrument executed by both the

SELLER and the BUYER or their attorney. If two or more persons are named herein as BUYER, their obligations hereunder shall be joint and several. The captions and marginal notes are used only as a matter of convenience and are not to be considered a part of this agreement or to be used in determining the intent of the parties to it.

26. Lead Paint Law

The parties acknowledge that, under Massachusetts Law, whenever a child or children under six years of age resides in any residential premises in which any paint, plaster, or other accessible material contains dangerous levels of lead, the owner of said premises must remove or cover said paint, plaster, or other material so as to make it inaccessible to children under six years of age.

27. Smoke Detectors and Carbon Monoxide Detectors

The SELLER shall, at the time of the delivery of the deed, deliver a certificate from the fire department of the city or town in which said premises are located stating that said premises have been equipped with approved smoke detectors and carbon monoxide detectors in conformity with applicable laws of the Commonwealth of Massachusetts and the City of Lynn.

28. Urea-formaldehyde Foam Insulation

The United States Consumer Product Safety Commission (CPSC) has banned the sale of urea-formaldehyde foam insulation having determined that it can present an unreasonable health risk to those exposed to it. SELLER(S) herein state that to the best of their knowledge, the property does not contain any such product.

29. Massachusetts Practice Standards

Any matter or practice arising under or relating to this agreement, which is the subject of a practice standard of the Massachusetts

Conveyancers Association, shall be governed by such standard to the extent applicable.

30. Buyer's Inspections

The BUYER represents and covenants to the SELLER that they have had the opportunity to cause the premises to be fully inspected by one or more inspection services and that BUYER is fully satisfied as to the condition of the premises and is purchasing the premises in "as is" condition.

31. Broker Indemnification

The BUYER(S) and SELLER(S) mutually warrant and represent to each other that they have not contacted any real estate broker or salesman in connection with this transaction and were not directed to each other as a result of any services or facilities of any real estate broker or salesman; except those brokers listed in Article 18 above. The BUYER(S) and SELLER(S) agree to mutually indemnify the other against and to hold harmless the other from any claim, loss, damage cost, or liability for any brokerage commission or fee which may be asserted against the other as a result of the other's breach of this warranty. The provisions of this paragraph shall survive delivery of the deed.

32. No Prior Sale Contingency

The BUYERS specifically stipulate that this agreement in not contingent upon the sale of BUYERS existing property and that BUYERS expressly waive such a contingency for purposes of qualifying for a mortgage.

33. Notice

All notices required or permitted to be given hereunder shall be in writing and delivered by hand or mailed postage prepaid, by registered or certified mail to BUYERS in care of their attorney as set out below and SELLER in care of their attorney as set out below, or in the case of either party, to such other address as shall be designated by written notice given to the other party and copies thereof shall be mailed by first class mail, postage prepaid, to

Buyer's attorney: [ATTORNEY NAME, ADDRESS, FAX, TELEPHONE]

Any such notice shall be deemed given when so delivered by hand or, if mailed, when deposited with the US Postal Service. Notice by facsimile to the fax numbers of parties' attorney as shown above shall be equivalent to the written notice described above.

FOR RESIDENTIAL PROPERTY CONSTRUCTED PRIOR TO 1978, BUYER MUST ALSO HAVE SIGNED LEAD PAINT "PROPERTY TRANSFER NOTIFICATION CERTIFICATION"

NOTICE: This is a legal document that creates binding obligations. If not understood, consult an attorney.

_____

SELLER　　[SELLER NAME]

_____

BUYER　　[BUYER NAME]

Appendix E

Collection Letter

RENT COLLECTION AND EVICTION POLICY   [DATE]

Rent is due on the first of the month. If you pay **before** the first of the month, you will receive a free large cheese pizza!

Rent is late on the 6th of the month. If you have not paid in full by the 5th of the month, you will be given a 14-day eviction notice. We do not chase tenants for rent. It is your responsibility to pay the rent on time.

RENT WILL NO LONGER BE COLLECTED IN CASH. Personal check, bank check, money order, or credit card is the only form of rent that will be collected by [MANAGER & TELEPHONE] effective [DATE]. If you mail a check or money order, mail it to:

[PAYMENT ADDRESS]

WE ARE NOW TAKING CREDIT CARDS. If you would like to pay with a credit card, fill out the form below and return it to [MANAGER].

If you do not have a credit card, but want to get one, you can call the following number. You might not know this, but some credit cards will give you money back for using them. They will pay you for paying your rent! We will only be taking MasterCard, Visa, and Discover.

Citi Credit Cards
1-800-950-5114
(TTY: 1-800-325-2865)

Bank en Español
1-800-374-9700
(TTY: 1-800-788-0002)

MBNA/Bank of America
1.800.932.2775
Monday-Friday 7:00 a.m. to 10:00 p.m.
Saturday and Sunday 8:00 a.m. to 5:00 p.m.

Advanta
1-800-780-3945

Capital One
1-800-695-5500

Discover Card
1-877-587-1605

If you have any questions, please contact us immediately at [TELEPHONE].

Credit card number _ _ _ _-_ _ _ _-_ _ _ _-_ _ _ _
expiration date: _____/_____

APPENDIX F

Tenant Application

Property Management
NAME
ADDRESS
CITY, STATE ZIP

Move-in Info
Property
Type:

_____

Deposit: _____ Rent: _____
Contract: _____ Move-in date: _____

Applicant Info
First Name: _____ Last Name: _____
SSN: _____-_____-_____ Birth Day: _____/_____/_____
Phone: (_____)_____ Cell Phone: (_____)_____
License: _____ Smoke?: Yes _____ No _____

Co-applicant Info

irst Name: _____ Last Name: _____

SSN: _____-_____-_____ Birth Day: _____/_____/_____

Phone: (_____)_____ Cell Phone: (_____)_____

License: _____ Smoke?: Yes _____ No _____

Others Who Will Be Living in This Property

Name: _____ Relationship: _____ Age: _____

Name: _____ Relationship: _____ Age: _____

Name: _____ Relationship: _____ Age: _____

Name: _____ Relationship: _____ Age: _____

Name: _____ Relationship: _____ Age: _____

Current Address

Address: _____

City: _____ State: _____ Zip: _____

Appendix G

Maintenance/Work Order

DATE REPORTED: _____

TENANT: _____

ADDRESS: _____

PHONE NUMBER: _____

REPAIRS NEEDED: _____

_____

_____

_____

_____

DATE OF DAMAGE/BREAKAGE: _____

DATE OF REPAIR BY LANDLORD: _____

COST OF REPAIR: $ _____

AMOUNT TO BE PAID BY TENANT: $_____

TENANT UNDERSTANDS THAT IF DAMAGES WERE CAUSED BY TENANT OR TENANT'S GUEST/ VISITOR, TENANT MUST PAY FOR ANY AND ALL RELATED REPAIRS. NOT DOING SO MAY RESULT IN YOUR EVICTION. IN ADDITION, CONTINUED DAMAGES TO YOUR APARTMENT MAY ALSO RESULT IN YOUR EVICTION IN ACCORDANCE WITH YOUR LEASE AGREEMENT OR TENANCY AT WILL UNDER MASSACHUSETTS GENERAL LAWS.

SIGNATURE OF TENANT: _____

This building has thirty-two units with two commercial storefronts. There is a washer and dryer on each floor, and you can see one of the cell towers on the front left of the roof.